# HOW TO WRITE A WINNING UCAS PERSONAL STATEMENT

**IAN STANNARD**

2ND EDITION

**The Daily Telegraph**

*How to Write a Winning UCAS Personal Statement*

This second edition published in 2010 by Trotman Publishing, an imprint
of Crimson Publishing, Westminster House, Kew Road, Richmond, Surrey
TW9 2ND

© Trotman Publishing 2008, 2010

First edition published 2008
Reprinted 2009, twice

**Author:** Ian Stannard

Designed by Andy Prior

**British Library Cataloguing in Publication Data**
A catalogue record for this book is available from the British Library

ISBN 978-1-84455-225-2

Typeset by IDSUK (DataConnection) Ltd
Printed and bound by in Italy by LEGo SpA

# HOW TO WRITE A WINNING UCAS PERSONAL STATEMENT

# Contents

| | | |
|---|---|---|
| **PREFACE** | | **v** |
| **ACKNOWLEDGEMENTS** | | **viii** |
| **PART ONE** | **Introduction** | **1** |
| **CHAPTER ONE** | No short cuts! | **7** |
| **CHAPTER TWO** | Why go to university in the first place? | **13** |
| **CHAPTER THREE** | What course to study and where? | **25** |
| **CHAPTER FOUR** | Your Personal Statement: getting started | **31** |
| **CHAPTER FIVE** | How to avoid a poor Personal Statement | **37** |
| **CHAPTER SIX** | The first section: your choice of subject | **43** |
| **CHAPTER SEVEN** | The second section: the subjects you are currently studying | **51** |
| **CHAPTER EIGHT** | The third section: your extracurricular interests and achievements | **55** |
| **CHAPTER NINE** | The final polish | **59** |
| **CHAPTER TEN** | CUKAS: How to apply to music conservatoires | **61** |
| **CHAPTER ELEVEN** | Answers to frequently asked questions | **67** |

| | | |
|---|---|---|
| **PART TWO** | **Academic profiles** | **75** |
| | Accounting | 76 |
| | American studies | 81 |
| | Archaeology and anthropology | 88 |
| | Biological sciences | 90 |
| | Business, banking, management and actuarial science | 95 |
| | Classics | 100 |
| | Computer science | 106 |
| | Drama and theatre studies | 110 |
| | Engineering (civil) | 114 |
| | English | 118 |
| | Environmental science | 122 |
| | Fine art and art foundation | 127 |
| | Geography | 134 |
| | Geology | 139 |
| | History | 145 |
| | Journalism | 148 |
| | Law | 153 |
| | Mathematics | 157 |
| | Medicine | 160 |
| | Midwifery | 164 |
| | Modern languages | 168 |
| | Music | 172 |
| | Nursing | 175 |
| | Oceanography | 179 |
| | Performing arts | 184 |
| | Philosophy | 189 |
| | Physics | 191 |
| | Physiotherapy | 197 |
| | Podiatry | 201 |
| | Psychology | 206 |
| | Sports and exercise science | 212 |
| | Theatre and performance design and technology | 216 |
| | Tourism management | 221 |
| | Veterinary science | 223 |
| **PART THREE** | **Further information** | **227** |
| | Good university guides | 228 |
| | Alternative guides | 229 |
| | General guides to subjects and course requirements | 229 |
| | Websites | 230 |

# PREFACE

ince the first edition of this book was published the world of higher education has moved on and the world has experienced the most significant global recession since the 1930s. A surge in university applications is putting extra pressure on applicants to achieve top grades in their exams. In the last application cycle there was an 8% increase, numbering about 42,000 students, in applications for full-time study at university – the biggest rise in eight years. The recession and rising unemployment were cited as prime factors in the late surge. The high number of applications will mean that pupils who are offered places on popular courses, or at prestigious universities, who do not attain their predicted grades will have less room for manoeuvre. It also means that the quality of the application will need to be first class in order to secure an offer in the first place.

2010 will also see the introduction of the new A* mark at A level. This has been introduced to help the universities discriminate between able and very able students. Too many students are now leaving with A grades, making the job of choosing the best students all the more difficult at top universities.

It remains the case that the Personal Statement is a pivotal part of any good application and for that reason the advice in this book has been updated to ensure that all the inside information is current and accurate. We have added journalism to the list of subject profiles, together with accounting, history of art, and sports science, and included a new FAQ section which will help anyone who is filling in the new-style UCAS application form.

I was delighted at the success of the first edition and hope that this updated edition builds upon that success and helps you gain the place at university that you covet.

It has been a privilege to work so closely with hundreds of young aspiring undergraduates over the last decade. Education reforms have come and gone, yet the essential principles of success remain the same. If you work hard at what you enjoy, take care to present yourself enthusiastically and articulately, and take the time to think about what you want from life, you will not go far wrong. Applying to university is not an exact science. Choices about where to study, what to study and whether to study are essentially personal. These personal choices will be influenced by your parents' aspirations, your background, your friends and your teachers. However, when push comes to shove, the choices you make are your own and your need to take responsibility for them.

You therefore need to be informed. This information also needs to be informed by current experience and reality, not 'what it was like in my day'! This is the purpose of this book and why I felt moved to write it. It will help you write a good Personal Statement and so present a good winning application to a university admissions panel. The advice in it is current and – importantly – driven by the experts, the admissions tutors who will read your application. They are the 'gatekeepers' who ultimately decide your fate. It is their views that count most in this competitive process.

My own views have been coloured by working at one of the UK's ancient schools, Christ's Hospital, for the last decade or so. Although it is an independent school, with able students, it remains one of the few 'needs blind' public schools in the UK. If we assess that a pupil has potential for greater things, we take that pupil and ask the parents to pay a fee that is commensurate with their ability to pay, which means that some may pay nothing. This is because the school is allied to one of the oldest educational charities in the UK and still remains true to its ethos, an ethos that was developed during the reign of Edward VI. As a result I teach pupils from all walks of life. Some are first-time applicants from their family to seek higher education and tick all the 'widening participation' boxes. Others are sons or daughters of Oxford graduates who bring their own unique problems to solve.

This mix has meant that I have dealt with the full range of issues that can arise in this area and have an idea what it is students and parents new to this process want and need to know. The Personal Statement is for many the scariest part of the application. It need not be so and this book will help to ease you through this part of the form so that you end up with something of which you can be proud.

Ian Stannard
March 2010

# ACKNOWLEDGEMENTS

I would like to thank a variety of people who have assisted me in the completion of this new edition. Writing is a process that I love but it is collaborative and without that collaboration would be impossible.

Let me start with the universities that have offered of their time and support. One of the major advantages that this book has is that it is written using material provided by the supplier – namely the departments who look to recruit new undergraduates. This inside knowledge means that it is not just about what I think but also about what they think too, which is far more important! Each department is mentioned by name in the book but I would like to thank Caroline Dimbleby at Essex in particular for her help. I am also grateful to Godfrey Cooper, my father-in-law, whose advice and proofreading is most gratefully received and to Alison Yates and her team at Trotman whose patience and professionalism makes the process far less stressful.

Finally, thanks to my wife, Jenny, and two children, Harry and Emily, to whom this book is dedicated, who put up with me working late at night and playing with the computer when I could be doing something else! Without Jenny's support in particular none of this would be possible.

PART ONE
# INTRODUCTION

**❝❝** The Personal Statement is a crucial part of the UCAS form: a marketing tool for your interests, talents, and accomplishments. **❞❞**

**QUEEN MARY'S, UNIVERSITY OF LONDON**

**T**he Personal Statement is probably the most important piece of writing that most students aiming to gain entry in higher education will complete outside of an examination hall. In an increasingly competitive marketplace, the supply of good courses in many areas of study is outstripped by demand. The result is that for some highly competitive courses, such as psychology, medicine, law, English, social work and physiotherapy the number of applicants can exceed supply by ten times.

Most universities do not have the resources to interview all good candidates. Indeed, you are unlikely to be interviewed unless you are applying to Oxford or Cambridge or for a medical course. Instead they rely principally on four pieces of information when deciding whether to offer the applicant a place:

**1** the student's academic record so far and their current academic profile: are they studying A levels, International Baccalaureate or an equivalent qualification?

**2** the student's Personal Statement

**3** the academic reference provided by the school or college

**4** the predicted grades that the school or college provides.

My experience of talking to many current admissions tutors is that they look first at the academic record and second, the Personal Statement. They do look carefully at predicted grades and the academic reference, but increasingly they base their opinion on the actual GCSE and AS grades achieved to date and the quality of the Personal Statement. Since the decision was made to make the academic reference 'open' rather than confidential, the references that were once candid are now increasingly bland or unwilling to say anything that might undermine the success of an application.

This point is tellingly made in a comment received from an admissions tutor at Nottingham University:

> ❝ We are somewhat concerned about some tutors overselling their students, exaggerating their predicted grades and abilities of the candidate so as to get them a good university place. Where the expected performance can be demonstrated or justified (for example, with overall grades or an upward trajectory in performance) the student's case is improved. This is especially important where predicted performance and current or previous performance appear to differ. ❞

Therefore, wake up and smell the coffee! It is hard to get a place at a good university and it appears to be getting harder every year. An unprecedented surge in applications by young people to start higher education in the UK in September 2009 has seen the number of British candidates rise by 10% from last year. Applications from the rest of the European Union are rising even more quickly, up by 16.4%.

Malcolm Grant, the Provost of University College London, was quoted in the national press in June 2009 as saying:

> ❝ We have never seen anything like the upsurge in applications, It is across all sectors, postgraduate, international and even our conventional UK and EU undergraduate applications. EU students have to be treated the same. There is a crowding out possibility – if you take an EU student it is a place that is not available to a UK student. We get superb overseas students, especially from France and Germany, and we must treat them on the same basis and offer them places on the same basis. They turn up here and they are dead keen to have come to London on their own initiative. They have studied English in a formal way and are pretty impressive. ❞

But with applications at record levels, many students have been disappointed. The proportion of applicants failing to get a place has risen. While the UCAS statistics do not specifically indicate how many UK applicants were disappointed, they show 156,315 applicants either withdrew their application or were unsuccessful in finding a university place. In 2008, 130,786 applications were in this category – 25,529 fewer than in 2009.

It is therefore vital that you follow these basic rules of thumb.

**Your UCAS application must be handed in on time and be free from errors.** There is a school of thought that says that an early application gives an applicant an edge. This depends on the policy of the university. Some offer places throughout the application cycle (normally September to mid-January) and others operate what is known as a 'gathered field' approach and wait until the closing date. However, in my experience most will offer a good candidate a place as soon as they read the application. So an early application cannot do any harm. Don't forget that Oxford, Cambridge, medical, veterinary and dental applications must be completed by 15 October.

**Your Personal Statement must sell you in a way that is compelling, engaging and well informed.** A lazy approach to this key document is fatal, particularly if you are applying to a course that is oversubscribed. A busy admissions tutor is looking for a reason to reject you as much as to offer you a place! In the real world, tutors will face a large pile of applications knowing that they are going to have to whittle them down to a shortlist. Don't give them an excuse to bin yours because of a poor statement.

**Your reasons for applying must be good.** Your statement must point to evidence that indicates that you understand the course content and have the skills to thrive in their department. This means taking time to do the research properly before doing anything else. I cannot emphasise this enough. You are fortunate to live in a world where up-to-date information can be accessed easily via the internet. Take the time to decide what you want to study, and why, with due care and attention. You cannot write a winning application and statement without understanding your enemy!

It is a myth that the statement is the hardest thing to write, although in my experience it is what causes 50% of the heartache. The other 50% is deciding what to study and where. Making decisions is tough and for many of you this is the first time you will be making a major educational decision without your parents being at the centre of the process. You should consider their advice, together with the advice gained from books such as this, your teachers, university prospectuses and your friends. However, in the end it is you who sign and send the form to UCAS. You must therefore take responsibility for its success and failure.

Do not despair. I am a strong believer in the phrase 'keep it simple, stupid' or KISS for short! This is the purpose of this book. I aim to make the process of deciding what and where to study and writing your statement less painful and more fulfilling. I have worked with thousands of students applying to universities all over the UK and have read more Personal Statements than I care to admit. If you follow the advice in this book, you will be well on the way to producing a statement and application that will win you the offer you want.

# CHAPTER ONE
# NO SHORT CUTS!

**Y**ou cannot write a good Personal Statement in isolation. The information you need to write it well is only gathered by careful research. This takes time but it is time well spent.

Think of the 'what', 'why' and 'where' questions that we often ask ourselves. You need to find out what you want to study, why this subject motivates you and then consider where you want to study. A common theme in all the conversations I have had with admissions tutors is that four things are vital:

- that you know what you really want from a university course
- that you can sell your enthusiasm for the subject you have chosen clearly and with confidence
- that you know what academic grades the departments are looking for: be brave but also realistic
- that the location you choose suits your personality and wider interests.

This is where the academic profiles (starting on page 75) will be so useful to you. Each one takes a different subject area and lets you know what studying that subject may be like, the qualities they look for in a good candidate, what to write and what to avoid in your Personal Statement and other tips to make your application stand out from the crowd. These were all written in collaboration with real admissions tutors and therefore do represent an inside guide to how to impress a busy academic tutor.

Here are some extracts from a range of subjects to whet your appetite!

This is what a tutor at Queen Mary's, University of London has to say about the skills or attributes that they look for in a good applicant for English:

> **"** Admissions tutors will always consider the level of attainment in GCSEs and predicted grades for A levels first of all. Many English courses now demand very high grades, simply due to supply and demand. It is not at all uncommon for candidates to be made offers of AAB or higher. Equally, it is not unusual for candidates to be rejected from one or more of their preferred universities. However, it is also possible to get into English courses with lower grades. Do your research carefully! **"**

> **"** The Personal Statement and school reference are then read for any signs that interest in English is not just a narrow product of quite enjoying it at A level. Tutors would hope to see indications of longstanding enjoyment, and an understanding that English at university will not be like three more years of A level English, but will be more demanding and unpredictable. We want to see evidence of wide reading and an appreciation of different literary genres. **"**

> **"** Good applicants demonstrate excellent academic potential, demonstrated by their strong A level or equivalent grades, and enthusiasm for further study. They show good time management and teamwork skills; the one to manage independent study successfully, the other to work co-operatively in seminars and group projects. **"**

All this information needs to be included in your Personal Statement or academic reference!

Here are some comments on what makes for a good Personal Statement for a potential physiotherapist from an admissions tutor at Brighton University.

It's really helpful if you have observed some physiotherapy sessions, to briefly describe your experience and explain why you would like to study it. You really need to describe something more varied than a personal experience of receiving physiotherapy – which shows that you have made an effort to see different aspects of physiotherapy – or at least have plans to broaden your understanding. Many departments do not look favourably at an overemphasis on sport. Most physiotherapists work in hospital settings and do not get involved in any form of sports-related injury or rehabilitation. **"**

It's always good to hear about your activities beyond the academic, particularly if you are interested in continuing them at university. Try and show a range of interests other than sport. We are interested in music, drama and other extracurricular pursuits, especially if they show evidence of individual leadership or teamwork skills. If you have had a job or done voluntary work make sure you explain something positive about the experience of interacting with people. **"**

Try and find a balance between self-promotion, explaining your recent experiences of work, social activities and school achievements. Overemphasis on any of these elements can skew your statement. **"**

You can read an example of a successful Personal Statement in Part Two.

## SUMMARY

A good Personal Statement is one that is written at the end of an exhaustive research process. Students who are right for the course, who have understood the demands of the subject and are ready to take on the challenge write winning Personal Statements.

Weak Personal Statements are under-prepared, written in a hurry and without the zeal that is evident when an applicant knows what they want and promotes themselves with confidence.

Before you even start to write your Personal Statement you need to ask yourself some searching questions and be prepared to work hard to find the answers. Good applications are often successful applications, and successful applications are informed and enhanced by good research.

What I mean by this is that when you send in your application, it is sent on the assumption that you consent to UCAS passing it on. This consent implies that **you** have done your research and not relied on hearsay! Too many students drop out of university in their first year or change their course when they arrive, because they were poorly informed from the outset. This is crucial, not least because it is expensive to go to university and you don't want to waste your money!

Informed consent is not easy. You need to devote a considerable amount of time to this process to prepare a winning application and Personal Statement. The bulk of a Personal Statement is a clear, convincing and enthusiastic statement of why you are passionate about that subject you wish to read at university. This passion and enthusiasm are hard to muster without a clear vision of what it is that you are letting yourself in for!

One good way to start is to answer these questions – make notes that you can refer back to later when we start to draft your statement.

**QUESTIONS TO ASK YOURSELF**

**Why do you want to study that subject and what evidence do you have that your interest is real and not superficial?**

This is a key component of the first part of your Personal Statement.

**Where do you want to study and why?**

Admissions tutors want to know that your reasons for studying a subject at their university are based on good grounds. Do you understand the demands of the course or the type of teaching and learning styles that you will encounter? This is something that ought to be addressed in a statement.

**What do you know about the skills and attributes that the admissions tutor is looking for and how will you convince them that you possess these key skills?**

Emphasise these skills in your statement.

**What evidence can you provide that supports your interest? This evidence must be more than just a list of what you have done at A level.**

A good Personal Statement will show evidence of wider reading or participation in activities that support and extend your knowledge and understanding of the course you have applied for.

**What do admissions tutors in your area of interest look for in a good statement?**

Go to the profile section first and if in doubt, email or telephone a tutor at a local university for advice. They are keen to hear from potential applicants, particularly those local to the applicant's home.

**What have your studies so far taught you about the course you hope to apply for – for instance, if applying to read chemistry, what have you done at A level or equivalent that sparked your interest?**

This is another key part of your Personal Statement and may be included in the first or second section.

| **What extracurricular activities do you undertake – do any of them give evidence of personal leadership, excellence or initiative?** | This is what you write in the final part of a good Personal Statement. |
| --- | --- |
| **What plans do you have post-graduation or are you planning a gap year?** | This is something that you may allude to in the final section of your statement. |

As you can see, there is a lot to think about before you start your first draft. I will start by asking you some questions about your motivation to study, your subject interests and what skills you have that you hope to extend at university. I will ask some searching questions that you may like to discuss with your family, friends or schoolteachers. I will also point you in the direction of some excellent books, websites and organisations that may help you in this initial process.

Only when you can answer all these questions are you ready to start the drafting stage. I suggest that you divide your statement into three distinct parts, working on each and then drawing them together at the end. Each part has its own emphasis and importance and a chapter of the book is devoted to each part in turn.

We start with some advice about research – why to do it, how to do it and where to look for expert help and guidance.

# CHAPTER TWO

# WHY GO TO UNIVERSITY IN THE FIRST PLACE?

I n your parents' lifetime, the number of students in full-time education post-18 has risen significantly. The government wants 50% of the British population to undertake higher education – this is far higher than the figures that attended in the past. In the 1980s, less than 20% of the population attended a British university. The increase in demand has brought with it its own problems. In the 1980s there was a large grant cheque at the start of the term for many; most students would eat well in the college refectory and drink enormous quantities of beer in the college bar. As soon as the money started to run out it was soup and a roll in the refectory and a beer that lasted all evening!

The only way to secure more money was the benevolent bank manager, and students who went overdrawn, as most students did without parental support, were not always given extended credit! It was rare to see students with multiple store cards and credit cards. There were few hardship funds, access to learning funds and no advice and guidance on budgeting; equally, there were no tuition fees either.

The debts and the numbers of students going to university were small but rewards were high to this élite. Because of the limited supply of graduates, employers were making highly attractive offers to students, and unemployment after graduation was unheard of. It was a huge incentive to go to university and, apart from modest borrowing from the bank or parents to supplement the grant cheque, the loss of income when compared with those going straight into employment after A levels was soon recouped from much higher starting salaries.

Today the financial implications of going to university and completing a three- or four-year course are a serious issue calling for full and proper consideration and consultation before you make the commitment.

## UNIVERSITY TODAY

The drive to increase the numbers entering higher education has resulted in sustained growth of degree places during the past 20 years. Students have to pay for their education and when they graduate it is becoming more difficult to obtain the higher-paid graduate jobs that were the norm before.

From the academic year starting in October 2009, students will have to pay tuition fees of £3,225 per year (compared to £3,000 per year in 2006) and students may take out a loan of up to £6,928 per year to help with the extra expenditure.

Students are running up debts in the order of £18,000 to £20,000 at present and with the increase in tuition fees and the continual use of credit cards, debts in the order of £20,000 to £22,000 are more than likely.

The reality is that nobody knows exactly what debt students will have on leaving university and for courses such as medicine, which has extended periods of study before graduation, the debts are likely to be higher. This makes it all the more important to keep a close eye on your finances by budgeting in order to reduce debt.

### For more information about student finance

UCAS website: www.ucas.com/students/studentfinance/

Ian Stannard and Godfrey Cooper, *A 6th Former's Guide to Money Matters*, ZigZag Education Publishers, http://Zigzageducation.co.uk

## SO WHY GO?

Essentially the reasons for this are varied. Here are some of the factors that students I have worked with have come up with.

- **To get a good job:** most professional careers now have a recognised graduate entry route. Although it is not imperative to get a degree to get a good job, there is an assumption that graduates are more likely to be employed. Of course, once you start your career, your success or otherwise will depend on your ability to do the job. A degree is just the key to the door; it does not always guarantee that you will enjoy accelerated promotion.

- **To please my parents:** many parents live vicariously through their children. In my experience they vary in their approach. Some parents are too pushy and expect their children to go to university, as this was their own experience. This is particularly true of parents who expect their child to get a place at Oxbridge or medical school. Parents who are non-graduates can be equally forceful about the need to get a degree and realise the advantages of a degree in career progression.
- **All my friends are applying:** this is another powerful pull towards university. This is particularly the case when the student's friends all aspire to higher education.
- **To better myself:** this group of students want to go to university to help them enjoy a better life than their parents were able to give them. Evidence does suggest that the most successful students at university will often be those who had to fight hard to get in, perhaps against the odds, for a variety of social or educational reasons. The Widening Participation model was established to work with and encourage this cohort of students.
- **I am not sure what I want to do for a living:** some students go to university to put off the inevitable life choice. They are unsure of what they want to do, so they go to university to give them more time to consider their options.
- **My chosen career requires me to graduate:** many degree courses, for example medicine, nursing, engineering, law, physiotherapy and veterinary science, are vocational and a degree qualification is an essential first step.
- **To make more money:** this is the most mercenary of all the motives but probably lies at the heart of most students' thoughts when contemplating three more years in education. From the Labour Force survey 2008, we are told that graduates in their twenties are likely to earn around £6,000 per annum more than non-graduates, and around 76% more than non-graduates in their forties. This is also confirmed by the Organisation for Economic Co-operation and Development (OECD), which found in an international survey that those with degrees in the UK will earn on average 59% more than those without degrees.

## PAUSE FOR THOUGHT

You need to ask some more questions and take notes of your answers to refer back to later on. These questions are often best debated with friends, family and teachers at your school or college. Don't be afraid to ask the opinions of others to help inform your own.

These are all important questions to answer **before** you start to write your Personal Statement. They force you to look at yourself critically and assess the real reason you want to stay in full-time education or perhaps not, and take some time out.

## Do you look forward to leaving school and beginning in higher education?

Leaving school can be an exciting and scary prospect. The certainties of school and college life are lost. You are used to a group of friends who you may have known for years, rules you understand (even if you hate them!), teachers who you understand how to manipulate and teaching styles that you are used to. Starting again in a new institution, away from home for the first time and with all the bills to pay yourself, can be daunting! Do not be afraid to express these fears and talk them through. You are not alone – far from it!

## Do you want to continue to study a subject that you are studying at school or college?

Most students study a subject at university that is in some way linked to their educational choices post-16. Even if you are not studying the subject directly, such as English, chemistry or maths, many will choose a discipline that builds on skills learnt at A level (or their equivalent): for instance, biochemistry or nursing, which both build on science skills learnt at school. This is important to consider when choosing the course.

## How will you show this transfer of skills in your Personal Statement?

Going to university is also the opportunity to do other subjects that you are interested to explore but may not have done before. Subjects such as archaeology, classics, philosophy, law, podiatry and management are open to you in a way that they may not have been at school. Here, the admissions tutors are not looking for evidence of existing A level knowledge, just potential and latent interest. For example, the classics tutor at King's College London makes it clear that they do not look for classics or Latin at A level but rather for skills picked up in most humanities or language courses:

> 66 As a good classics (etc) applicant you will have the same general skills and attributes as any good humanities prospect: enthusiasm, self-motivation, a desire to learn, an appetite both for different perspectives and for challenging questions. The King's College London admissions team hope to see applicants who enjoy independently exploring new topics, whether in the library, the museum, or the field; people who want to engage with new problems and techniques, and to get behind the clichés of mass-media versions of ancient myth and conflict. 99

## Do you want to live away from home?

Unlike in mainland Europe, UK students have traditionally moved away from home to study post-18. This is a trend that seems to be in modest decline, with an increasing number of students choosing to live in their home towns. This is particularly true of undergraduates from poorer families with little history of higher education. Reasons for this vary, but the financial advantage of home life is one major factor. It can cost in excess of £120 per week to live in a hall of residence in London, which is a major expense for most students starting a degree course. That said, my strong advice is to live in halls of residence in the first year if at all possible. Living at home in the first year can make it hard to make friends and will cramp your style!

## Are you willing to pay for this opportunity and what is your attitude to debt?

It is not cheap to study at university. There are a number of costs that need to be met and for most students there is a shortfall between the income they receive from grants, bursaries and loans and the total cost of living. However, the advantages of a university degree are significant and money should not put anyone off giving it a try. Do consider the cost of living when looking at location. It is far more expensive to live and study in London than Hull! You will learn to live in debt as a student but this is quite manageable if you follow some simple tips.

- ▶ **Learn to budget:** look at your outgoings (spending habits) and look at your income. As much as possible try not to leave too big a gap between the two.

- **Avoid credit cards and store cards:** these are often a disaster for students and can lead to major problems, including court action, if you cannot make the payments. I know more than one former student who cannot get a mortgage now because of credit card debt when they were at university. This is real life now, not school rules and detentions!
- **Expect to have to get a job** in term time and in the holidays. This is true unless you are applying to Cambridge or Oxford where the short terms and high workload make it inadvisable to get a part-time job in term time. Colleges have funds to help students in need.
- **Keep a check on your spending on luxuries,** including alcohol and fast food. Try to learn to cook for yourself as this is almost always cheaper than pre-cooked microwave meals. It is also sometimes cheaper to live in catered halls as the food is provided for you. As long as you eat it, this will cut your bills!
- **Avoid unnecessary expenditure such as car insurance.** Cars at university rarely make sense unless absolutely necessary. You become a taxi service!
- **Make sure that you have personal insurance** away from home and that you get a TV licence if you have a TV in your room. A hefty bill after a fire, or a fine after a visit from the TV licence van, is not in most students' budget plans!

A small number of my former students have made all these mistakes in the last few years. For good advice, consult one of the many good guides to student money available in the shops or online.

## Are you an independent learner?

All my research indicates that the ability to show evidence of this skill is vital. If possible, mention your independent learning in the statement with evidence to support your claim.

The learning and teaching style at school is very different from that at university. There is a lot more emphasis on personal learning and initiative. This lack of direction and teacher contact is often a major source of disappointment for new undergraduates. Admissions tutors are looking for evidence in the Personal Statement that you have the drive and personal initiative to cope in this sort of environment. To give you an example, here is an extract from a profile written by admissions tutors at Surrey University and Durham University, both of which admit students into modern language courses.

> Most language courses are taught using a variety of different methods. Some lectures are conducted either in English or a foreign language. These would normally be lectures to support modules in history, business or law for instance. They would also see students in small seminars, where the language was spoken and discussions take place about literature, politics or current affairs. Students are also encouraged to give presentations in the foreign language. Departments also use language laboratories and audiovisual material, from films to foreign documentaries. In most departments, including Birmingham and Surrey, teaching methods therefore aim to promote 'student-centred learning'. This means that they encourage you to be responsible for your own learning and for the organisation of your work, and to set high standards and goals, such as near-native competence in your target languages. The role of the teacher in this process is to encourage and support you, to guide your learning and to engage in an exchange of ideas with you. 𝅻

How would you show these skills in your Personal Statement?

### Do most of your friends expect to go to university and do your parents want you to continue in full-time education?

Your friends and parents will not have to do the work you are asked to do at university. By all means listen to them but be yourself. You cannot just do what others want you to do. If your gut feeling is that you need time away from full-time education before applying, then take that time. Taking a gap year is one way of giving you this space to think. However, I would normally suggest that unless you are dead set on not going to university, you apply for a deferred place (you take a gap year before you start) rather than apply post-A level.

## Are you clear about the career you want to pursue and do you expect to have to get a degree to start this career?

Some careers such as medicine, architecture, nursing and engineering require vocational degree qualifications. Your Personal Statement needs to show evidence of your commitment to these careers before you apply. Have you completed work experience and if so, what did you learn? Have you taken time to speak to practitioners or even worked for companies in that industry part time?

## What reasons might you have for not going to university?

Think about what you might do if you do not go to university. Are you going for good reasons? If not, and you are not committed to a course, this will show in a Personal Statement that lacks clarity and personal enthusiasm.

## Are you the first person in your immediate family to consider going to university?

The government is very keen, as are most universities, to recruit more students from currently under-represented backgrounds. Research suggests that students who meet these criteria are less likely to apply:

- students whose family is from socio-economic groups III to V (this means that your parents work in semi-skilled manual/non-manual jobs or unskilled jobs or are unemployed)
- people with disabilities
- mature students: students who are over 23 years old
- people from certain ethnic minorities.

If you think you are a student from one or more of these backgrounds, you may qualify for additional support in preparing your application from university 'widening participation' officers. They often run taster courses, advice clinics and other incentives to encourage you to apply. If in doubt, ask to speak to an officer at one of the universities in which you are most interested. Cambridge University has a special access scheme for students from these backgrounds. It is worth applying through this entry scheme if you expect to be a student with the potential to get in.

## Should students from these groups indicate this on their application form or Personal Statement?

This struck me as an important question to ask the admissions tutors who collaborated with this book. If there was an advantage to be had if you were considered a widening participation applicant, this ought to be made clear in your Personal Statement or academic reference.

The answers we received from the universities varied. Some were adamant that they did not look at the socio-economic group at all. They simply accepted pupils based on academic potential regardless of their background. Others did look at the school to see what success it had when admitting students, and this may favour a borderline candidate. A good candidate from a school with little or no history of sending students to university would be given extra credit.

Others advise you to be explicit if you are from a group that meets the widening participation criteria. You should mention it if you are the first in your immediate family to attend university or if you are in a family that is economically disadvantaged. This is perhaps best done in the final paragraph of your Personal Statement and this is what I encourage my students to do. The school should also allude to this in their academic reference.

The following are direct quotes from a number of different university departments.

> **"** The Institute of Archaeology very much supports the Widening Participation agenda, and has undertaken numerous activities to encourage applicants from a wide range of backgrounds, including taster days, masterclasses, and events in National Archaeology Week. As a discipline, archaeology has traditionally attracted a very broad spectrum of applicants, including a high proportion of adult learners. **"**
> **UNIVERSITY COLLEGE, LONDON**

**“** We've always encouraged widening participation and invite a large proportion of people who apply to us to come to our auditions. It can be helpful to see an explanation that someone has not had the opportunities to take part in a range of acting roles simply because of their personal circumstances. This would not in any way debar from audition. **”**
**LIVERPOOL INSTITUTE OF PERFORMING ARTS**

**“** The University of Southampton's approach to widening participation is focused around encouraging, recruiting and supporting people who have the ability, enthusiasm and potential to succeed at university, but who come from groups that are currently under-represented in higher education and the University of Southampton itself. The University also offers bursary schemes to support its widening participation agendas, meaning that one-third of its students receive a University of Southampton Bursary. We do not currently take into account in the admissions process whether or not a student has a family history of higher education, with the exception of the BM6 Medicine programme. **”**
**UNIVERSITY OF SOUTHAMPTON**

All admissions tutors recognised that some issues that the applicant may want to raise that were pertinent to the application may be too private for a public document. Such issues could be expressed in a letter sent direct to the admissions office of each university. Too few applicants disclose this sort of information and this is detrimental to them and their application. All letters sent would be considered in confidence. Such letters should be supported by medical opinion, social work reports or other third party agency testimonials, where such support is appropriate. *(You are advised not to mention anything in your Personal Statement that you would not want read by too many people – this is the beauty of the supplementary letter.)*

**Note:** these letters should not be sent until **after** the application has been sent to UCAS and the applicant has received the letter of confirmation from UCAS.

## Do you have any special educational needs?

In my 2009 survey, no university indicated that they were concerned about special educational needs (SEN) disclosures. Such students will not be prejudiced in any way and indeed they will find that extra support is available to them when at university. There is no harm in mentioning in your Personal Statement that you have a particular SEN, particularly if you have overcome this and been successful.

From 2009, applicants were obliged to enter details about SEN on the UCAS form, even if simply confirming that they had none.

## What happens next?

The final stage of research before you start to write your statement considers the two most important questions:

1. what should I study?
2. where should I study?

# CHAPTER THREE
# WHAT COURSE TO STUDY AND WHERE?

**B**efore you start making an application and writing your Personal Statement, I want you to take some time to consider what it is you want to study and where. Many students just 'end up' at university without giving any serious thought to the nature of the course and location.

First, write down your answers to the following questions – you will refer to them again when you start to write your statement.

- List at least four reasons why it is important for you to go to university (in order of importance to you).
- Have you a particular subject or course in mind?
- If your answer is yes, can you write down some of the factors that influence your choice? In particular, think about the skills or attributes you possess that support your interest.
- If your answer is no, can you at least isolate the skills you have that you want to enhance and develop at university? These might include literary, mechanical, design, mathematical, artistic or sporting skills. It is clearly worthwhile playing to your strengths.
- Have you a clear career path in mind? Will this career require any qualifications that you can gain at university or college?
- Do you want to live near your home or would you be willing to move a long way away? Is location an important factor in your decision-making?
- Do you have a university in mind as your first choice? If so, what reasons can you give that support this choice? Do you know that the course requirements meet your expectations and academic potential?
- What about the other choices? You can make up to five in total, unless you are applying to medical, dental or veterinary school where you can only apply for four.

## WHAT TO STUDY?

You need to really know yourself and know the departments you hope to persuade to accept you. You must do your research and make it clear in the application and your Personal Statement that you have done this thoroughly. As you will see in the academic profiles, often admissions tutors refer to students applying with little understanding of the demands of the course. These applications and Personal Statements are more often than not consigned to the reject pile.

To research universities effectively, you can:

- use the excellent UCAS website (www.ucas.com)
- read books and websites (listed on pages 227–232)
- carefully read the websites of the universities and take the chance to visit them.

You will live there and study there for three years, so it is foolish to commit without ever walking the streets of the town or peering into the libraries and halls of residence.

## THE UCAS WEBSITE

The UCAS website (www.ucas.com) is an excellent site, full of useful advice. It has a comprehensive course search facility that allows you to access every course that is offered in the UK through the UCAS system. It allows you to compare courses and find out more about the nature of the courses.

Do use the course search facility as an initial sift. Look at the 'entry profiles' that have been compiled by all the universities. These give a good insight into what they are looking for in a good candidate.

## STAMFORD TEST AND UCAS-ENDORSED CENTIGRADE

The Stamford Test is a short questionnaire that can help to match your interests and abilities to possible higher education subjects. Many students find this extremely helpful when trying to make up their minds.

The test is extremely easy to use and I recommend that all my students do the test as part of their research activity. To do it, you need to register with UCAS.

Another popular and UCAS-endorsed test is 'Centigrade', which is designed and promoted by Cambridge Occupational Analysts (COA). Centigrade goes into much more detail, matching a student's interests, current academic grades, preferred degree subjects and likely range of UCAS tariff points scores to direct them to up to eight course areas. Once you have answered the questionnaire, COA will send you a detailed bound report with well-matched selections. Centigrade can be completed online or using a paper questionnaire. The cost is £20 for a full colour printed personal report (approx 48 pages). For further information phone COA on 01362 688722 or go to www.centigradeonline.co.uk.

## WHERE TO STUDY?

There will be many reasons why it is inappropriate or appropriate to apply to a particular university – these include academic grade expectation, cost of living, course content, proximity to home, graduate employment prospects and location (rural vs. urban; campus vs. non-campus). All these factors need to be teased out before you start to write your statement.

My students often ask what the right university is for them. Here is my answer which I trust will help you compose your own. In short, the best university is the one that best suits the individual student!

It is the university that offers you:

- **a course that is interesting:** make sure that you apply for a course that meets your needs and that equally you do not apply for a course that does not. A Warwick admissions tutor remarked to me recently that he was amazed at the number of students who simply applied because of the 'name' of the university, rather than because the course suited them. Such applicants often failed to gain a place as it was clear that they had not done their research
- **a good quality of teaching:** look at the information you can find on the excellent Guardian Education website (http://education.guardian.co.uk). League tables are not the be-all and end-all, but they are a good place to start
- **a favourable geographical location**
- **a realistic and achievable conditional offer:** it is clearly not appropriate to apply for a course where the expected grades

significantly exceed your grade predictions and previous academic record

- **a good graduate employment record:** very important, particularly in the current economic climate
- **a range of excellent facilities**, not least affordable accommodation.

## Choosing a course that is interesting and has good quality teaching

When doing your research, the following tips are useful.

- Check the research and teaching rating for the relevant course on the latest league tables. League tables are a good place to start, but do not reject those whose research rating is lower than four. Tables are useful but they need to be treated as starting points, not ends in themselves.
- The 'premier league' of the British university system includes the Russell Group universities. They are the ones with the best research ratings overall, the best reputation with employers (normally) and highest kudos. Most commentators suggest that the following are the 'premier league' (not all are in the Russell Group): Birmingham, Bristol, Cambridge, Cardiff, Durham, Edinburgh, Glasgow, Imperial, King's London, Leeds, Liverpool, LSE, Manchester, Newcastle, Nottingham, Oxford, Sheffield, Southampton, St Andrew's, Sussex, UCL, Warwick and York.
- The best course for you may not be at one of the so-called 'best' universities. You need to consider other factors, most notably employment prospects, course content and location.
- Look at some of the books available to help you such as Brian Heap's *Choosing Your Degree Course and University*. He does a lot of the hard work for you, giving a brief summary of each institution and their courses. It is updated every two years and published by Trotman. It is not cheap, so look for it in a school, college or local library.
- Ask for your own copy of all the relevant prospectuses. You can order them via email by going to the universities' websites. Online prospectuses are also first-rate and are usually updated before each admissions cycle. They can often provide more up-to-date information than the expensive-looking paper copies. They also provide details of open days and taster events. These 'taster' events are particularly useful when preparing the first part of your Personal Statement.

## Further research opportunities

You will find many books, websites, magazines and prospectuses to help you make these two vital decisions. My favourites are in the Further Reading section.

However, I am now going to assume that you have done the reading, asked the questions and thought about your options. We shall now start to write your statement that will hopefully be part of your passport to the course that you crave!

**FACTORS IN YOUR CHOICE**

| | |
|---|---|
| **The right geographical location** | Do you want to live away from home? There are personal development factors to be gained when living away from home and this can prove significant when seeking a job. |
| **An offer that realistically you are going to achieve** | You need to balance optimism with pragmatism. Ask yourself what you really expect to achieve and what evidence from past performance you can point to in your statement and academic reference to support this. There is no point applying for a course that you cannot reasonably expect to get into with your predictions or subject profile. |
| **A good employment record for recent graduates** | If you are clear about what you want to do after university, the subject must provide a suitable basis for that career. |
| **A range of excellent facilities, including accommodation** | The facilities offered by universities are similar: they will all have a library, a sports hall and careers service. However, if you require a specialised facility, then this is a factor to consider. A climber is not advised to go to East Anglia if he or she wants access to mountains! |

# CHAPTER FOUR

# YOUR PERSONAL STATEMENT: GETTING STARTED

**Y**our Personal Statement is, I believe, the most important piece of writing that you will complete outside of the examination hall. For that reason alone, it is vital to take the time to get it right. Most universities in the UK do not have the resources to select via interview. Cambridge interviews almost all candidates whose applications are considered worthy of further exploration; Oxford does the same in some subjects but 'deselects' between 20% and 25% of applicants for some subjects. Other universities do interview, but they tend to be for highly competitive courses, vocational courses such as medicine, veterinary science or nursing. Artists and architecture applicants are often interviewed to examine their portfolios, and drama and music students should expect an audition.

The application form is, therefore, the only medium that most students can use to sell themselves. Note my use of the word 'sell'. This is deliberate. The British are often reluctant to sell themselves well: they think that it is either boasting, evidence of an over-inflated ego or worse!

This is a mistake. You need to write in a way that is persuasive, emphasises your strengths, minimises your weaknesses and essentially 'sells' you (the applicant) to the reader (the admissions tutor). The admissions tutor is the 'gatekeeper' and if your statement is not engaging, undersells your achievements or is poorly constructed then the tutor will be less inclined towards offering you a set of keys!

## HOW DO THE UNIVERSITIES USE YOUR STATEMENT?

The University of Leicester student support service suggests on its website that your Personal Statement gives you the opportunity to:

- help the university find out about you and your suitability for the course they have to offer

- present your goals, experiences and qualifications in the best possible light
- demonstrate your writing ability
- distinguish yourself from the other applicants.

**Note:** if a candidate is unfortunate enough not to achieve the grades of the offer, often the admissions team read the statement again if they are toying with taking an applicant anyway!

## THE BASICS

Most UK students use the UCAS online system Apply (www.ucas.com/students/apply/) to process their application. UCAS expects you to enter the Personal Statement directly into the application and limit the word count.

You cannot write more than 4,000 characters or 47 lines of text in a standard font. I recommend that you use font size 12 (Times New Roman). This is important as the page is reduced from A4 to A5, so smaller text can become illegible. You cannot use italics, bold or underlining, as these will not be transferred into the Apply package. Inexplicably, neither will accented characters such as é.

Don't waste your time on fancy formatting. Apply will not allow indented lines or coloured fonts. Apply does allow all the common punctuation marks and the following symbols:

! £ $ % ∧ & * () @ # ~? – =

but **not**:

© ∞

I also recommend disabling the 'auto format' feature in Microsoft Word as this can mean that dashes and quotation marks are removed from the submitted Personal Statement.

The Apply software does not have a spell-checking facility. You should write your statement using a word-processing package. Once it has been *thoroughly* checked for spelling (make sure you have set UK English as your default!), punctuation and grammar, you can cut and paste it into Apply.

our statement should answer these questions succinctly and in a style that is
ngaging and informative. You need to have evidence to support your claims, so
hink about what evidence you might provide.

## irst section: your choice of subject

- Why have you chosen to read the subject at university?
- What is the background to your interest in the subject?
- For how long have you had this interest?
- What particular areas of your studies appeal most and why?

ese questions are particularly pertinent if you are applying for a vocational
gree such as medicine, nursing, law or physiotherapy.

ention any relevant work experience, summer employment or voluntary work
at supports your application. This is vital when applying for all medical-based
urses where they will expect you to have arranged suitable work experience.
r instance, you will not be interviewed for a physiotherapy course if you have
t done at least two weeks' work placement.

- Have you completed any relevant taster courses in preparation for your
  degree course such as Headstart, VETSIX or Medlink?
- Have you taken part in a NAGTY (National Academy for Gifted and
  Talented Youth) course?
- Have you spent any time on a residential course run by a university?
- What did you learn?
- How useful were the courses?

se are very good selling points that you must emphasise.

- What are your career aspirations?

ition this if it is pertinent to the subject you wish to read.

In my experience, many applicants leave the first draft of the statement un
very last moment, sometimes weeks or months after they have chosen th
course. Teachers are busy, too, and although sixth-form UCAS tutors are
experienced, leaving things to the last minute can lead to errors slipping t
This is more often than not the fault of the student, so start early and keep
school or college deadlines!

## WHEN TO START

This is an easy question as the answer is succinct – early! By that I mear
your lower sixth-form year. I ask my students to write a draft in the gap b
the end of their AS exams and the end of the summer term. This forces

- make some early decisions about what to study
- look at themselves critically
- begin the research that is vital to prevent poor choices in the lo
- do something constructive rather than vegetate while waiting fo
  term to end!

It does mean that they return in the autumn with something to go on. T
autumn term is very busy and anything that puts you ahead of the gam
worthwhile. This is particularly true if you need to apply early – by 15 O
places at Oxford, Cambridge and medical, veterinary and dental schoc
want to apply for an Oxbridge choral or organ scholarship, you will nee
done in the first week of September!

A good Personal Statement will probably take three weeks to write. So
leave it to the last minute.

## THE STRUCTURE OF YOUR STATEMENT

| YOUR STATEMENT: QUESTIONS TO ASK YOURSELF | | |
|---|---|---|
| **First section** | 40% | Your choice of subject to study university |
| **Second section** | 35% | The subjects you are currently |
| **Third section** | 25% | Your extracurricular interests a achievements |

## Second section: the subjects you are currently studying

- What particular interests do you have within your current AS and A2 (or equivalent) courses?
- How have they helped you choose the course?

Mention all of your subjects and briefly explain which parts of the course you have found most interesting and why. However, where a subject is directly relevant to the subject you are hoping to read, greater bias must be given to your enjoyment and skills in that discipline.

- What evidence of wider reading or experience beyond the syllabus can you produce, particularly within the subjects directly relevant to your chosen subject?

**This is crucial and often grossly underestimated.** Many applicants simply do not read anything beyond their textbooks. This is not a successful way to convince an admissions tutor that you deserve to spend three more years studying with them to degree level! You should name books, articles or media events that have inspired or challenged you, and be able to explain why. Listing a series of books without evaluation of at least one main theme is mere name-dropping. If you are likely to be called for interview, be prepared to discuss some of the references at length. In other words – do not lie!

## Third section: your extracurricular pursuits and skills

This section focuses particularly on your extracurricular pursuits (both in and out of school or college). You can also emphasise important skills you possess, such as leadership, initiative and personal skills.

These final paragraphs should give evidence of the following areas.

- **Extracurricular subjects:** what subjects are you studying outside the curriculum?
- **Other achievements:** these achievements should be substantive and show that you are both able and dedicated. High grades in music or

drama exams, Duke of Edinburgh's Awards, Combined Cadet Force or Scout awards are all worthy examples.

- **Leadership potential:** give evidence of your leadership potential, how you were selected (elected?) and what you learned from leading your team.
- **Inside school:** have you held positions of significant responsibility, for example head boy or girl, house captain or prefect, chair of the student council, debating society, enterprise teams, Target 2.5 interest rate challenge, or sports captain.
- **Outside school:** local political party work, charity work, church choir, uniformed organisation, young church leader, non-school sporting achievement.
- **Other successes:** details of significant other successes you have enjoyed – these may include community or charity work, for example, running the London Marathon, or anything else that sets you apart from the couch potatoes with their eyes glued to Sky or the latest PS3 game!
- **Gap year:** mention any gap year plans you have, accentuating the positive advantages of such a gap year for your future vocation. Most universities are happy to offer you a deferred place but Oxbridge tends not to encourage deferred applications for mathematicians and that is also true of other major universities. This is something to research and consider carefully before you fill in your UCAS form.

I have deliberately divided the statement into two large sections and one smaller section. Universities are places of academic study and research. Most admissions tutors are highly educated, committed (sometimes devoted) to their subject and keen to work with like-minded undergraduates. They want to recruit students with other interests too. However, being a good rugby player, musician and pool player will not cut much ice if your academic profile is weaker than the next applicant's.

## CHAPTER FIVE
# HOW TO AVOID A POOR PERSONAL STATEMENT

**T**hese tips are all drawn from experience and as a result of direct advice from admissions tutors. You should read them together with the academic profiles on pages 75–226. They will give specific advice about different academic disciplines and are therefore well worth reading carefully.

- **Clarity:** avoid waffle, generalisations and poor sentence construction. Be precise and concise. Say what you mean in a clear, uncluttered manner.
- **Tone:** avoid humour – this is a professional document. Weak applicants misjudge the tone of the document they are writing.
- **Style:** avoid 'text-speak', colloquial slang and language that may offend.
- **Length:** use the full amount of space that you can. This is probably the most important document you have written outside of an exam hall in your life. If you cannot say enough about your passion for the subject and why you are an interesting person to teach to fill the full 47 lines, what does that say about you?
- **Enthusiasm:** don't be dull – dry, uninspiring prose indicates a dry, uninspiring applicant. Appear very interested, enthusiastic and well read with an informed judgement about what the course is about.
- **Sell yourself:** promote your achievements and potential.
- **Language:** avoid poor spelling, grammar and punctuation. This is crucial if you want to be taken seriously in any application you make, be it to university or for a job. If this is a personal weakness that you are aware of, ask someone else to proofread your statement. This is particularly relevant if you are an international student or if English is not your first language. Applications without spelling mistakes have been known to receive offers; those with mistakes may be self-penalising.

- **Be yourself:** don't try to be the 'ideal' applicant. They want to get to know you, not the person you are pretending to be. After all, if you kid them into taking you and then start the course, you may find that you are not cut out for it when you start. This is both demoralising and expensive if you subsequently leave.
- **Avoid plagiarism:** do not copy anyone else's Personal Statement. You will read exemplary Personal Statements in this book, written by successful applicants. Learn from them and the advice given by the tutors who picked them. Please do not copy them – this gives a false impression to the tutor and is fraudulent. You are asked to sign that everything in the application is correct to your knowledge. Any lies or plagiarism uncovered will be treated seriously and may jeopardise your application. Most universities now employ tools to detect plagiarism among their own students.

UCAS is now employing a system called 'Copycatch', which will compare every application submitted with thousands posted on websites and over a million submitted in previous years. If three sentences or more – 10% of your statement – appear to have been copied, the form will be passed to staff for further scrutiny. Be warned! There is evidence that a significant proportion of students do lift material directly from other applicants' Personal Statements. Not only is this fraudulent: it is also unfair to you as in the final analysis you want to go to a university that suits you, not the person you are trying to imitate!

Before we start to construct your statement, here are some final thoughts for you to consider.

The aim of this guide is to provide you with information that is clear, current and supported by the universities. A successful Personal Statement and UCAS application as a whole is one that stands out.

## MORE QUESTIONS TO ASK

These questions are more focused on the drafting stage. You need to write your answers down so that you can look at them again, together with the other notes you have already made.

**What subject/subjects do you want to study at university? List the reasons you are drawn to this subject.**

This is one of the key elements of any successful Personal Statement. You need to have a pithy and well-written statement of why you want to study your chosen subject with some supporting evidence that will back up your claims.

**Who or what has influenced you the most to study your subject?**

For example, is there something that's triggered your interest in the subject – did you go to a lecture or have a really good teacher? Or if you've just read a book, mention that. But don't make it up. If you have not had any particular 'eureka' moment, and it is just a subject that you've loved at school, then say so.

**What wider reading have you done to support this application?**

Do not just mention the books you have had to read in the A level course! What magazines, newspapers and internet sites do you read or visit to extend your knowledge?

**Have you attended taster courses or undertaken work experience? If appropriate, list the plays, films or TV programmes you have seen and say how they have influenced you.**

This evidence should be presented clearly in the opening paragraph of your Personal Statement.

**What research have you undertaken that has led you to this degree choice?**

I just want to be sure that you have done the research necessary to make this decision. Do you know the course content well and does this meet your own skills, interests and aspirations?

**What subjects have you studied so far that support this application? Do you require any particular subject at A level (or equivalent) to be accepted?**

This is a vital part of a successful Personal Statement. Please do not fall into the trap of applying for a course that you cannot get into to because you lack the minimum academic credentials. Many admissions tutors I spoke to complained about this weak and lazy approach which was often exposed in the Personal Statement.

**Can you list the skills that you have developed in each course you are studying (or have studied) that support your application?**

These may be analytical, mathematical, problem solving, written, oral or simply subject-specific. For instance, the study of maths may have taught you analytical skills, design may have given you spatial awareness, or English the ability to read and write quickly and persuasively under pressure. This is a key component of the second section of a good Personal Statement.

**What coursework projects or extended pieces of work have you been asked to do or completed as part of your course (if applicable)? What skills have you developed or do you expect to develop?**

Universities are keen to hear about skills that you may have already developed that are linked to university teaching and assessment styles, particularly independent learning, research and extended essays.

| | |
|---|---|
| **What are your future intentions and goals (after school and university)?** | This is relevant information to include in the final paragraph. If you are unsure, do not worry, as this is 'nice to know' information but by no means critical. You may want to mention any gap year plans but only if they will enable you to be a more proficient or able student as a result: for instance, foreign travel to a country whose language you hope to study. |
| **What extracurricular accomplishments do you wish to draw to the attention of the admission tutors and why?** | These are important to mention in the final section of your statement. Concentrate on a few significant achievements, particularly if they involve leadership roles, personal initiative, team-building skills or the attainment of recognised qualifications. |

## SUMMARY

You will now have answered many questions that are all relevant to your Personal Statement. You now need to look again at the notes you have made of your answers.

At this stage try to draw the notes into three groups that suit the three distinct sections of the Personal Statement. To remind you, the first stage is broadly speaking a clear explanation of why you want to study that course together with evidence to support this interest. The second section is a summary of the skills and attributes that you have acquired through the study of your A levels or their equivalents, with special emphasis on the skills that are most relevant. The final section is a summary of your extracurricular pursuits, placing particular emphasis on the activities that emphasise your leadership potential or personal initiative.

Look again at the advice given in Chapter Four for further help. Once done, you can start the first section of your statement.

# CHAPTER SIX
# THE FIRST SECTION: YOUR CHOICE OF SUBJECT

**F**irst impressions really do count. Look at the successful Personal Statements provided by universities later in this book. Giving your Personal Statement a strong opening will engage the reader's attention from the outset. Common mistakes include the use of clichéd and overused sentences in the introduction. For example, you should avoid starting your sentence with the following:

'I have always wanted to study. . .'

as this is patently not the case; or

'My passion has always been for. . .'

which is a similarly unlikely claim for any 18-year-old to make! You should instead imply an interest in your chosen course. You need to quickly show the admissions tutor that you have a genuine interest, and this requires the use of specific examples.

Look back at your answers to the questions in Chapter Five – what examples can you give?

Perhaps it is the books that you have read beyond the syllabus, the lecture you attended in your free time, the taster course you paid to attend in the holidays or the work experience placement you have either completed or arranged.

You could refer to a leader in the field of your interest who has inspired you – for instance, a philosophy and politics applicant could write about Plato's *Republic* and its views on the structure of democracy and justice.

You may refer directly to an event or person in your life that has inspired you – for instance, a student of mine recently wrote about her interest in medicine being linked to the fact that she has lived with a genetic disease. Her personal investigation into this illness – its aetiology and likely development – plus repeated exposure to medical professionals was the genesis of her desire to study medicine.

You will also need to draw attention to any work experience that is relevant and most importantly what you learnt while undertaking this experience.

## WORK EXPERIENCE

It is vital to mention relevant work experience in the opening half of the Personal Statement if the course requires it. Admissions tutors ask applicants to get relevant experience for two main reasons.

**1** **To demonstrate commitment to your career choice:** just enjoying *Holby City* does not justify a strong desire to work as a doctor. A committed applicant to medicine must demonstrate a commitment to the community, which could mean working as a hospital porter during the holidays, attending a hospice as a helper over six months, spending at least one day in a GP's surgery or taking the time to arrange a meeting with a consultant.

**2** **So that they can be sure you are going into this career path with your eyes open:** you've seen the reality of the job, warts and all, and it hasn't put you off. A potential applicant to teacher training needs to be aware that pupils are not always well-behaved and that teaching involves a great deal of time-consuming administration. They learn this by sitting in with a primary class and talking to teachers at their local senior school. In my experience, schools are nearly always willing to offer a potential undergraduate the opportunity to do this if they write well in advance.

The most common courses that expect work experience are:

**Medicine:** the Medical School at Sheffield University has the following advice for potential applicants.

❝ A good Personal Statement will include information on your relevant work experience. Medical schools expect applicants to have a range of work experience for two reasons. Firstly, this demonstrates that you have a realistic insight to the profession – you are after all committing to a lifetime career when you apply to study medicine. It is important that you have an understanding of the complex nature of a doctor's role, as well as being aware of the highs and lows of the profession. ❞

❝ Work experience is also important in enabling you to develop (and to demonstrate that you have) the relevant skills and qualities that are essential to becoming a good doctor. A few examples are listed below.

- communication skills
- a sense of service to the community
- a sense of responsibility
- self-insight
- energy
- enthusiasm
- perseverance
- ability to overcome setbacks
- ability to work independently
- experience of working with diverse groups. ❞

❝ We recognise that it is not always possible for students to obtain work placements in a medical environment given the limited availability of volunteer placements in hospitals and similar clinical settings now. However there are many areas related to medicine in which you can gain experience. Some examples of these are listed below.

- paid or voluntary work experience in a residential care home, hospice or similar
- working in a youth centre or working with young children
- participating in community volunteering schemes
- shadowing a GP or other medical practitioner to gain an insight to their role, responsibilities and the complexities of healthcare
- working with a diverse range of people (whether on a paid or voluntary basis). **"**

> **"** Participatory work experience (not simply observing, but a 'hands on' role) is extremely valuable. Many applicants arrange to undertake paid or voluntary work as a healthcare assistant. Whatever work experience you have, it is important that you reflect effectively on this in your Personal Statement. **"**

Most medical schools expect at least two discrete work experience placements. Many hospitals now do not offer ward-based work experience to those under 18. Try your local hospital's human resources department but do not be surprised by a refusal. You are also quite likely to be able to arrange a visit to your local GP to have lunch with a doctor to discuss his or her career and recent issues in the NHS that may come up in an interview. A well-crafted letter to your own GP can pay dividends. Mentoring younger pupils in your own school can help your interpersonal skills, and work with disabled teenagers promotes empathy.

**Dentistry:** my experience is that dental surgeries are generally happy to have a well-chosen potential dentist in their surgery for a few days. They might expect you to cover in reception, observe some routine procedures, talk to the hygienist and in return help out with the filing! I recommend contacting your own dentist, preferably including a reference from your school or college testifying to your genuine interest and academic potential.

**Nursing and midwifery:** Queen Mary's, University of London (QMUL) suggests that care homes and hospices are excellent settings in which students can find out if they are really suited to this type of work. For midwifery, applicants should contact their local hospital's midwifery service manager to arrange experience in the maternity unit – most universities will require a minimum of one day's experience, if nothing else, so that students can learn that being a midwife is not about babies! It's actually about looking after the mothers.

**Physiotherapy:** similarly, the QMUL website says that physiotherapy is probably one of the most competitive courses a student can apply for, so getting work experience is essential. Most jobs are in the NHS, so experience in this setting should be the student's main priority, even if they are aiming to work in sport (a growing, but still very small, area of physiotherapy work). It is sometimes possible to get a paid (rarely) or voluntary physiotherapy assistant post in an NHS hospital; failing that, shadowing a chartered physiotherapist is the next best thing.

**Veterinary science:** there are only seven vet schools in the UK and competition to get in is fierce, although the myth that you need all A*s at GCSE needs exploding! Potential applicants need to spend time with both small and large animals and this may be problematic if you live in an urban environment.

However, most vet surgeries are used to written requests for help, so start there. Think laterally – you may live near a children's farm; they look after animals and you could volunteer to work there. One successful student who I knew did this at a local children's farm from the age of 14. She is now a successful vet in London. If you own a pony or horse, the stables will have qualified professionals on hand to advise.

**Teaching:** most degree courses that integrate Qualified Teacher Status (QTS) will interview and expect some relevant work experience. Evidence that you have worked with children elsewhere is also important – so get involved with local scout groups, youth clubs or programmes working with children in the holidays such as the Barracuda organisation. You will need to undertake an enhanced disclosure test to work with children.

**Note:** all of the above will expect you to undertake an enhanced disclosure test or Criminal Records Bureau check (CRB) and, in the case of medicine, be inoculated against certain diseases (especially hepatitis B) before you start the course.

Here are some examples of excellent opening paragraphs from real Personal Statements that were all successful in gaining offers at Oxford, Cambridge or other leading universities.

**THE ARCHAEOLOGY AND ANTHROPOLOGY APPLICANT**

Having spent the first 13 years of my life in Kenya, it was always going to be a culture shock when I moved to England four years ago. My time in both countries has given me a better perspective on the globe on which we live. From a young age I was fascinated by the human race. Through visits to Samburu and Maasai settlements and day-to-day living in Nairobi, I began to realise the great diversity within human culture, further revealed by trips to Kenya's Islamic coast and then by a move to England. Here I experienced a very different outlook and a very different way of life, captured well in Watching the English by Kate Fox. My own life has triggered a need to understand more about the reasons for these differences. I hunger to learn about 'the self' while studying 'the other', to know who we are and how we got where we are. Anthropology is the obvious route to this knowledge.

**THE CLASSICS APPLICANT**

Classics is for me both fascinating and mind-stretching. I view its insistence on total understanding of complex grammar, creative literary criticism, stringent philosophical analysis, and various other disciplines, as an essential beginning of what I hope to carve into a scholar's life. My first encounter with Greek tragedy lay with a verse translation of the Oresteian Trilogy whose formal structure, elegant language and emotional intensity struck me deeply. I was amazed to find myself laying aside all my atheistic ideals, instead fearing the wrath of ancient deities. Sophocles similarly forced me to care about King Oedipus; the end to the plot, known to the audience, the reader and Tiresias, made further reading an unpleasant prospect, whilst the righteousness of Oedipus' struggle to help his own people made me continue out of hope for a different fate. I was thus compelled to witness human suffering from the reflectively remote yet intimately shocking perspective of the theatre and truly learnt the meaning of catharsis from those four plays.

**THE ENGLISH APPLICANT**

The study of English literature has undoubtedly shaped the way I think. Philosophical deliberation has been a necessity in the reading of both Paradise Lost and Hamlet, for example, with Milton's attempts to 'justify the ways of God to men' being pertinent to Hamlet's lamentation of the human condition and what he perceives to be the sheer inevitability of suffering through life. The exploration of the historical contexts behind these two works has been equally absorbing, with the similarities between the God of Paradise Lost, and the king condemned by Milton, lending a particularly revealing insight to Milton's own disposition. Indeed, through learning English, I have encountered a wide range of disciplines, and it is the extreme diversity offered by the subject that makes it so wonderful and informative for me; rigorous analytical thought is developed through practical criticism, while the flexibility and creativity of writing is cultivated through essay and prose composition.

## THE HISTORY APPLICANT

EH Carr called history 'an unending dialogue between the present and the past', a concept that has always fascinated me. Each age will see something different in the past as being 'significant'. History tells us not only about the nature of the past, but about the nature of the age in which history is written. For example, the way current historians interpret the Crusades is informed by the present situation in the Middle East but also needs to take into account the views of historians contemporary to those cataclysmic events. The concept of a 'clash of civilisations' needs to be tested in both the present and in the past.

## THE MEDICAL APPLICANT

The aim of every branch of medicine is to alleviate avoidable suffering in the human body and mind. Caring for a person's needs by providing a cure, managing a condition or maintaining general health is a role that I look forward to, for its intellectual stimulation and emotional fulfilment. Medicine is not stagnant; developments in patient care, technology and new treatments will leave me constantly challenged and needing to update my knowledge and skills. I hope to be able to contribute to the body of research, hopefully into infectious diseases in the developing world and gynaecology, two areas of particular interest to me. I am drawn to medicine by my analytical and inquisitive mind, as a profession that presents questions answered using a range of tools as well as innovative thinking.

## THE MODERN LANGUAGES APPLICANT

To me, language in its essence represents a key to another culture, opening the door to a world of new experiences. Since childhood I have been amazed by the vast difference in thinking and lifestyle on opposite sides of the Channel. Visiting France annually with my family, such contrasts have fascinated me, and in studying the French language I have attempted to become more than just an observer, but rather a participant and appreciator. The wealth of cultural thrills that this has imparted is my greatest motivation in taking my study of French to university level, as well as expanding the possibility of such opportunities in the study of Spanish.

## SUMMARY

Draft this first section carefully using a word processor. Make sure that you ask advice from a teacher or tutor and that it is read by at least two people who can check it for quality and possible error. Do not worry too much at this stage about length. It is easier to précis a long well-written piece then to pad it out. You will in the end need to cut it down to meet the length requirements but this can wait until later.

# CHAPTER SEVEN

# THE SECOND SECTION: THE SUBJECTS YOU ARE CURRENTLY STUDYING

 our Personal Statement must proceed in a logical succession from one thought to the next. The body of your Personal Statement should lead in a convincing way from the introduction to conclusion.

The second section should focus on the skills you have already gained while at school or college. When talking about your educational background, do not just mention what is clear from the rest of your application. They can read elsewhere how many GCSEs you got.

The primary focus should be on any A level courses that are directly relevant to your choice of degree. The historian should talk about his or her History A level first and at greatest length. Focus on what you have learned and what skills you have honed.

When you introduce your other AS or A level subjects, it is wise to draw attention to the ways in which your other subjects have complemented your skills and learning in the principal subject.

- Talk first and foremost about the subjects that you are currently or have recently finished studying that are directly relevant to your choice of degree. How have they helped you choose the course?
- Do not repeat what an admissions tutor can read elsewhere: telling them how many GCSEs you have got is irrelevant.
- Do mention, however, if you have any very high marks in AS or GCSE papers: this sets you apart from the rest. By this I mean that you may have obtained 100% in one paper or full marks in your extended or project work.
- Mention any coursework or extended work that you have completed that suggest that you are capable of independent learning. This is an important facet of university teaching and learning.

- Mention the other subjects that may not be directly relevant, but have enabled you to gain useful skills.
- Quote books, magazines, websites or courses that you may have read or attended. However, do not lie as this can be exposed at a later date and lead to rejection.

A good example of this can be found in these extracts from real Personal Statements.

### THE CHEMISTRY APPLICANT

Currently I am reading Why Chemical Reactions Happen by James Keeler and Peter Wothers, which is challenging my understanding of what I have learnt and taking me beyond the boundaries of the A level course, at the moment into wavefunction and the associated quantum mechanics. Although the material is at a higher level than my current studies I can use my knowledge and understanding from the work I have done so far to get to grips with more complex ideas. It has taught me to think objectively and formulate my own ideas from the information provided. Alongside chemistry I study medieval history and biology and have already gained an A at A level mathematics. Although chemistry is by far my favourite subject I also have a compelling curiosity about other areas of science, some of which biology has helped to satisfy. Studying human biology, in particular learning about how our bodies work, is fascinating, although I enjoy biology most when we study processes that involve using chemical knowledge, such as respiration. Over the years I have won four prizes in science, including ones for chemistry and biology this year. Medieval history has been valuable as there is no textbook so a lot of research must be undertaken outside of class, using contemporary and modern sources. This independent learning is crucial in allowing me to develop skills which will aid me when studying at degree level.

### THE HISTORY APPLICANT

My other AS subjects have complemented history well. Reading Joyce's Dubliners made me aware of the social context of a country about which I knew little; at A2 I hope to cement my understanding of the relationship between Ireland and England. Studying The Merchant of Venice and King Lear for coursework was simultaneously challenging and interesting on account of the fact that they both showed, or implied, various Jacobean beliefs and attitudes (such as the microcosm and macrocosm), which informed my understanding of prevailing attitudes held towards monarchy. I came to realise that writers may subtly change or subvert conventional forms of literature for dramatic effect, as in Merchant of Venice, where I paid particular attention to Antonio, whose plight, in my view, turned comedy to tragedy.

In music I became interested in the way Mozart used the rise of the middle class in Austria towards the end of the 1700s to his advantage. My composition took a variation and theme structure, using a variety of composers for inspiration ranging from Haydn to Stravinsky. Finally, having always had a true passion for pure maths, I was thrilled by the discovery of imaginary numbers and matrices in the AS course.

**THE MATHEMATICS APPLICANT**

As part of my A level Mathematics coursework I chose to use computer programs to develop various numerical solutions to equations. I enjoyed using software such as Excel and an online graph plotter. This led me to begin to appreciate how computers can help deepen one's understanding of mathematics as well as being a useful problem-solving tool. I think delving more deeply into the studies of computers will enable me to apply mathematics in a wider range of situations such as in physics and modelling in economics.

Due to family circumstances I spent a year studying in Hong Kong in 2007 where I took an accounting course which I greatly enjoyed and it gave me some ideas about what is involved in a career in accountancy. Mathematics plays an important role in accounting: first in making the necessary calculations and then in interpreting the financial data. Accounting has sparked a general interest in business. I enjoy analysing how the firms put all the input factors together to produce goods at the lowest cost and highest margins. Studying AS Economics also made me realise the complexity of the global economy. The large amount of graphical interpretation and data interpolation has allowed me to understand the essential importance of having fundamental mathematical skills.

**THE MEDICAL APPLICANT**

Biology has made me appreciate the complexity of life processes like respiration and photosynthesis. I find the biochemistry part of these processes, such as glycolysis, intriguing as it covers ideas that I have learnt from chemistry as well. Finally in philosophy I have been introduced to important ideas about how the mind and body are connected, as well as looking at key ethical dilemmas related to medicine, including euthanasia and abortion. I am also taking critical thinking as an extra AS level in my spare time. This is teaching me how to analyse data and arguments, which will be important in making impartial decisions in a clinical setting.

**THE MODERN LANGUAGES APPLICANT**

While at school I have gained eight academic prizes, including three for French and two for Latin. My study of Latin has been particularly useful for setting up a framework within which to learn languages, as well as for its rich history and literature. In English, I have nurtured a love for literature and developed analytical and evaluative skills. Studying history at AS helped me come to a greater understanding of the foundations of our European culture, as well as similarly furthering analytical and evaluative techniques.

# CHAPTER EIGHT

# THE THIRD SECTION: YOUR EXTRACURRICULAR INTERESTS AND ACHIEVEMENTS

**T**his is the final paragraph and should focus on your extracurricular pursuits. Although your academic potential is at the front of their minds, admissions tutors do want to recruit students who will bring other skills to the department and university as a whole. They are looking for someone who is academically motivated but not a couch potato.

You need in this section to attempt to show some distinct skills or personality traits. Here are the key skills that admissions tutors tell us they look for:

- persistence
- independence
- self-motivation
- leadership
- maturity.

Think now about what you do outside the classroom. What are your primary extracurricular pursuits? How have these pursuits helped you develop the skills that admissions tutors are looking for?

Add a concluding sentence or two. This will tie everything together. Integrate all the information gathered in the above paragraphs and finish on two positive sentences. The closing sentence must be powerful and succinct.

- Emphasise personal attributes that might include organisational skills, punctuality, sensitivity, responsibility, initiative, efficiency, communication and empathy. Where you mention one of these, give an example of what you have done to expose and develop this attribute.

- Mention any subjects that you are studying outside the formal curriculum, particularly if they are academic in their focus or lead to nationally recognised qualifications.
- Mention the extracurricular activities that you have undertaken. Don't just write a list. Concentrate on two or three activities that emphasise your personal qualities, such as leadership skills, initiative, sporting success or debating skills. The Duke of Edinburgh's Awards, Young Enterprise scheme and Combined Cadet Force or Scouts are all particularly good examples.
- Emphasise any roles that you have held that were significant: particularly if you were elected or appointed by a senior teacher – for example, prefect status, captaincy of a sports team or elected head of an activity.
- Mention career plans or gap year plans: make sure that your gap year plans accentuate the positive advantages of such a gap year for your future vocation or university career.

Here are some examples of extracts from good final paragraphs that proved to be successful.

### THE ENGLISH APPLICANT

I greatly enjoy playing sport, and have represented the school for the past two years in the football and cricket 1st XIs, and the rugby 2nd XI. In 2007 I spent two weeks helping at Bushfire Orphanage in Uganda, an experience I found both challenging and greatly enjoyable. I am also greatly interested in writing, and have proofread novels for Caroline Lawrence (a children's author), as well as proofreading a script for Bradley Quirk, a proofreader at the UK Film Council.

### THE GEOGRAPHY APPLICANT

Travel constitutes for me a real excitement, whether through school trips to the volcanoes and glaciers of Iceland and the eroded coast of Malta with its hugely exciting opportunities for scuba diving, or on journeys with the National Children's Orchestra to the Czech Republic and the county youth orchestra to Cyprus. Such travel has given me much food for thought on both economic and physical issues that impinge on globalisation. I have recently accepted an invitation to travel to Australia as a gap year student, mainly to teach hockey and other sports, an opportunity that would not only enhance my knowledge of geography, but also improve my leadership skills.

Another popular ending is one where you opt for a little self-promotion.

Overall I believe I have the necessary (academic/intellectual) ability, motivation and stamina to cope successfully with the demands of this subject and look forward to hearing from you in due course.

## THE HISTORY APPLICANT

I have taught myself GCSE Chinese, captained our successful school chess team for several years and completed the Silver Duke of Edinburgh's Award. I also have an active interest in politics and served as editor of our school political journal for a year. Debating is a particular passion of mine, and I will represent my school this coming year in the MACE competition.

## THE MEDICAL APPLICANT

My extracurricular commitments are significant and include representing the school at the highest level in football and rugby, serving as house captain and now school prefect, which not only involves working as part of a team but carries with it responsibility for others and leadership, offering younger students peer support. These skills came together when I volunteered at an old people's care home project, opening my eyes to the needs of the elderly in our community. I believe I excel at this because I am a non-judgmental person who empathises with others and understands the importance of having someone to listen to them. I am committed to a long-term career in medicine and am well aware of the unique demands of the role.

## THE NATURAL SCIENCE APPLICANT

Outside the classroom, I am in the 1st XV for rugby, and we recently went to Australia on tour and won all six matches. My passionate and driven nature allowed me to raise the funds and take my place on the tour. I am also undertaking my Gold Duke of Edinburgh's Award after having achieved Bronze and Silver. I also enjoy taking to the stage from time to time and played Bottom in the school's production of A Midsummer Night's Dream.

At university I plan to work to achieve my employment potential and expand my love and knowledge for chemistry. I have a strong desire to go into research chemistry and develop new compounds; most likely drug discovery or maybe even research into new materials. The reason I am so enthralled with the research aspect of chemistry is because I know that there are endless possibilities for discovery of new and useful compounds due to the advances already made by humans. Being a part of this scientific advance would be a privilege and honour that I am wholeheartedly willing to work for.

## WIDENING PARTICIPATION

In Chapter Two I talked about the widening participation agenda to which all mainstream universities have signed up. Essentially, the aim is to encourage applications from students who are from social groups that are under-represented in UK universities. These include:

- students from schools with a poor record of sending students to university
- students from families whose parents are in semi- or unskilled employment
- students who are the first in their family to attend university
- mature students
- students from certain ethnic backgrounds.

I advise you to allude to this, if it applies to you, in the final section of your statement. It is not clear to what extent it will influence admissions tutors. However, it can do no harm at all and at best may help persuade a tutor to take you if the decision is split.

A possible ending is reproduced here from an actual statement that helped win a place at medical school.

To study medicine is a dream that I have had since a small child, a dream that I am close to realising regardless of the fact that I have not enjoyed the benefits of an education in a school with greater experience of sending students to medical school. If successful, I will be the first in my family to attend university and this is an opportunity that if offered I know that I would grasp and not let your faith in me down.

# CHAPTER NINE

# THE FINAL POLISH

 great Personal Statement is a work of art, not a hastily written paragraph or two. It takes time to research, plan, draft and then redraft. Do not be afraid to redraft many times.

Use the three drafts that you have begun and, if you have not already done so, word-process your handwritten thoughts and begin the final drafting process.

The total length of the statement is 4,000 characters or 47 lines of text in a standard font. This is important, as the page is reduced from A4 to A5, so smaller text can make it illegible.

You need to consider the following when you redraft.

- **SPAG (spelling, punctuation and grammar):** do not be guilty of poor SPAG. If you are, the impression you give is poor. As I intimated earlier, ask someone who is a competent proofreader to check this carefully.
- **Present yourself in the best possible light:** make sure that your statement presents your goals, experiences and qualifications in the best possible light as well as demonstrating your writing ability. Have you mentioned the books you have read beyond the demands of the syllabus? Have you presented your work experience in the best possible light?
- **Get rid of any repetition or wasted words:** do not say what is already apparent elsewhere in the application.
- **Avoid waffle, generalisations and poor sentence construction:** be precise and concise. Say what you mean in a clear, uncluttered manner.
- **Avoid passive writing:** rewrite sentences that use the phrases 'has been' or 'was'. These are words that are good to cull if you need to précis something that is too long.

- **Avoid the word 'I' as far as possible:** save the word 'I' for when you need to write a short sentence that is full of emphasis such as 'I am a hard-working, conscientious and ambitious student.'
- **Length:** most of my students find the hardest part of the statement writing process lies in the careful précising that is necessary when it is 50 characters too long. This is a skill that requires time and effort. If you are really struggling, ask for advice from a teacher or fellow student who you know to be a good writer.
- **Be yourself, not the 'ideal' applicant:** they want to get to know you, not the person you are pretending to be. You will spend three years studying that subject. Be sure that it is what you want, that you sell yourself well but fairly and that when you pass the exams in August and win that place you know that it is the right place for you.

Good luck!

# CHAPTER TEN

# CUKAS: HOW TO APPLY TO MUSIC CONSERVATOIRES

**C**UKAS is the online application process that is similar to UCAS and it is found at www.cukas.ac.uk. CUKAS is UCAS-owned and the service is designed to provide the facilities to research on and apply for practice-based music courses at the following UK conservatoires.

| | |
|---|---|
| ◗ Birmingham Conservatoire | www.conservatoire.bcu.ac.uk |
| ◗ Leeds College of Music | www.lcm.ac.uk |
| ◗ Royal College of Music | www.rcm.ac.uk |
| ◗ Royal Northern College of Music | www.rncm.ac.uk |
| ◗ Royal Scottish Academy of Music and Drama | www.rsamd.ac.uk |
| ◗ Royal Welsh College of Music and Drama | www.rwcmd.ac.uk |
| ◗ Trinity College of Music | www.tcm.ac.uk |

It offers a potential applicant a range of research tools and an online application form.

**Note:** not all UK conservatoires use CUKAS at the moment. Currently the Royal Academy of Music (www.ram.ac.uk) and the Guildhall School of Music and Drama (www.gsmd.ac.uk) do not use CUKAS and have their own application form and audition process. Please contact them direct via the internet or telephone to obtain the latest prospectus and application form.

This chapter will provide you with a sound understanding of why students apply to a conservatoire, how to apply online (including what to include in the Personal Statement) and what to expect at audition.

# POINTS TO CONSIDER

## Why study at a conservatoire?

Conservatoire education is suitable for any talented musician who is particularly interested in performance, conducting or composition. They teach to a professional standard, combining practical and academic study in an environment that is steeped in musical history. Many of the teachers are leaders in their field and the UK is fortunate to have some of the finest conservatoires in Europe. Study in a conservatoire environment enables excellent networking and developmental opportunities for all musicians regardless of their specialism or musical direction.

Conservatoire students have the opportunity to conduct, perform or have their music performed on numerous occasions. Many of the performances are public and the students often find it is possible to earn money while at college playing at private parties and other functions. The range of music teaching available is vast, including jazz, orchestral, operatic, musical theatre and choral.

Students study for three- or four-year undergraduate degrees (BA and BMus) as well as postgraduate programmes such as MMus and PgDip.

## What are the entry standards?

As you can imagine, competition for places is high. Your traditional academic standards play 'second fiddle' to your performance standard. Each conservatoire has its own academic and performance demands. However, I will use information provided by the Royal College of Music (RCM) to give you an idea of the demands likely to be placed on you and any other applicant. Most of this information is pertinent to all applicants but you are advised to look carefully at the prospectuses of the others.

The RCM currently has the following minimum entry requirements for the BMus (Hon):

- A level Music at grade C or above (most students achieve grade A or B), and either
- a second A level at grade E or above, or
- two AS levels, both at grade C or above (not including Music).

Music Technology is not accepted as a substitute for A level Music, but can be your second A level or one of your AS levels.

If you are not taking A level Music, but still wish to apply to the Royal College of Music, you may still be considered if you can demonstrate an appropriate level of musical knowledge and literacy. You may be tested or interviewed at audition to ascertain this.

Alternative entrance qualifications which are accepted instead of A levels are:

- three Scottish Certificate of Education (SCE) Higher Grade passes, one of which should be in Music
- advanced general national vocational qualifications (GNVQs)
- BTEC qualifications
- European or International Baccalaureate or other equivalent
- international qualifications.

## What about auditions?
The Royal College has the following audition format.

- Auditions/interviews at the RCM are approximately 15–20 minutes long.
- For some instruments and for voice you may be asked to perform at a second audition on the same day.
- For set pieces see the Audition Pieces section of the online prospectus – www.rcm.ac.uk/Studying/How+to+Apply/Audition+ Pieces.
- Technical work (for example, scales and arpeggios) may be required of some instrumentalists.
- Sight reading may be required of all performers.
- An accompanist can be provided by the RCM if required, but you are strongly advised to bring your own accompanist, with whom you will have worked in preparation for the audition.

**Please note:** each institution has its own audition procedure. Please research this information carefully. The CUKAS site has a guide to auditions which can be downloaded from this site – www.cukas.ac.uk/documents/ CUKASAudition.pdf.

## When can I apply to CUKAS?

You can start an application in the July prior to attending the college the following year.

# THE APPLICATION PROCESS

## How many conservatoires can I apply to?

Up to six in one application cycle.

## What costs are involved?

The cost of the application is similar to UCAS, £15. In addition you will be asked to pay audition fees. These vary from institution to institution.

## Can I apply to CUKAS and UCAS in the same year?

Yes. Indeed, you are encouraged to do so as competition is so fierce that you need options to fall back on. You can apply to read music at university but there is nothing stopping you applying for something entirely different and then making up your mind at a later date. Keep your options open!

## What should I include in a Personal Statement?

The advice is broadly similar to UCAS Personal Statements, except conservatoires are far more interested in your musical skills. Emphasise why you have chosen the courses you have listed. Unlike UCAS applications, each conservatoire will know where else you have applied. Bear that in mind. You should mention:

- what local, national or international orchestras, choirs or chamber groups you are currently performing in, for instance National Youth Orchestra, National Youth Choir or European Union Youth Choir
- your experience in composition and conducting
- the music and composers who have inspired you so far
- any masterclasses you have attended, whether you have been involved in junior training programmes and any other gifted and talented initiatives
- what your career plans are, post application (if known)
- any non-accredited skills and achievements that you have gained through such activities as Duke of Edinburgh's Awards, Young

Enterprise or ASDAN (Award Scheme Development and Accreditation Network awards)

�, your sports, social or leisure interests
�, your gap year plans, if appropriate. You can apply for a deferred place.

As with all Personal Statements, heed this basic advice.

�, Make your interest in the subject evident in the opening few paragraphs with clear evidence supporting this from your study so far. You are writing for a tutor who shares this passion and wants to teach students with a genuine love for the subject. This may not always be possible, but whether it is or not, it is vital that the reader believes that you have thought about this application carefully and have good reasons to believe that you will thrive at that institution and department.
�, Avoid spelling, punctuation and grammar errors. Get your statement proofread by someone who is competent to do so.
�, Take advice where possible from a teacher who knows about the subject that you are hoping to apply for.
�, Avoid plagiarism or lies.
�, Emphasise your current skills and attributes, both academic and non-academic, in a positive and emphatic manner.
�, Treat it as a very important piece of prose that deserves your best efforts: take your time to get it right and when it is, be proud of it and ready to defend what it says if you are called to interview.

## How to fill in the application form

The form is completed online and in many ways it resembles the UCAS Apply system. The CUKAS site provides comprehensive advice and you should refer to www.cukas.ac.uk for more details. There are strict deadlines, so start as soon as possible and certainly start to prepare audition pieces with your music teacher(s).

## CUKAS letters

CUKAS only sends three types of letter to applicants during the application process.

**1** **CU2 Welcome letter:** this is sent when they have processed an application.

**2** **CU6 Replying to Offers letter:** if applicants receive one or more offers, once an applicant has received decisions from all their conservatoires, CUKAS sends a letter asking them to reply to their offer(s) by a given date. Applicants may only be able to accept one offer as their first choice, or they may be able to accept two offers and state their first and second choices. The number of offers an applicant can accept will depend on the type of offers.

**3** **CU12 Guaranteed Unconditional Place letter:** this will be sent to applicants when a place at their first choice has been confirmed, or if they do not meet the required conditions at their first choice, when a place at their second choice has been confirmed. Applicants will be asked to contact the relevant conservatoire if they do **not** wish to take up the place.

# CHAPTER ELEVEN

# ANSWERS TO FREQUENTLY ASKED QUESTIONS

**T**hroughout the last ten years I have been asked hundreds of questions about how to prepare a winning application to UCAS. This short chapter will attempt to offer answers to many of the most common. Many of the questions relate to filling in the form, so you might want to read this while completing an application online through Apply. Others are more general but still relevant to the needs of most applicants.

## APPLYING TO UNIVERSITY
### What are the best universities?
In short, the best university is the one that suits **you** the best! It is the university that offers you:

- a course that is interesting and meets your academic needs
- a good quality of teaching
- the right geographical location
- an offer that you are realistically going to achieve
- a good employment record for recent graduates
- good facilities.

Take the time to make up your mind and make sure the information you base your decision on is relevant, accurate and preferably based on a visit to the university. Have a look at the Further Reading chapter to find more places you can go for guidance.

### Should I go on visits and open days?
You should not commit yourself to three or more years at a university without having a good look at it and making sure you will feel comfortable there. One way of doing this is to take a trip during school holidays and to see as many places as possible.

Universities and colleges also have official open days. These can be a mixed blessing: thousands of school pupils milling around and all kinds of shows turned on to try to capture their interest. However, if you go with clear aims and questions in mind you can learn a great deal.

Attending faraway open days, and interviews too, can be horribly expensive. You should think carefully about exactly how many universities you need to visit. All university and college open days are listed in UCAS publications and on individual university websites. Apart from the cost of travelling to open days, there is also the fact that you will miss valuable teaching time in school.

## Should I apply to Oxford or Cambridge?

Competition to gain admission to Oxford and Cambridge may be fierce in terms of academic requirements but there are fewer applicants per place than for many other universities. In the arts, around 26% to 28% of the applicants will be successful in getting a place and in the sciences the figures are 28% to 30%. The growing numbers of qualified candidates from throughout the world compete for the places and this in part ensures that high academic attainment is needed for entry. It is no longer the case that those with less strong academic grades can compensate by being a more rounded individual through excelling in activities outside the classroom. Academic ability is paramount.

Therefore only pupils with the strongest academic qualifications should consider making an application. Three A grades at AS, a string of GCSE As and A*s and three A2 grade A predictions are regarded by Oxford and Cambridge as the **minimum** requirements for consideration rather than as guarantees of admission. The successful candidates, from among hundreds of applicants who meet these threshold requirements, are those who demonstrate a knowledge and interest in their chosen subject which far exceeds the normal requirements of their AS and A2 syllabus. Indeed, at the time of writing Cambridge has made it clear that it will expect applicants to gain a new-style A* in the A2 that most closely mirrors their academic choice. Oxford, on the other hand, has made it clear that it will not expect an A* until at least 2012! This adds to the academic demands on potential applicants.

Only those applicants who in their own time and on their own initiative have completed reading and research in addition to that required by their teachers have any realistic chance of admission. The universities establish this initially from the Personal Statement and it is tested at the selection process at the universities (see Chapter Seven).

However, at the same time as these universities are attempting to cultivate an intellectual and academic élite, they are also making every effort to extend access to young people from all economic and social backgrounds. The focus to encourage state school pupils to apply has now led to the charge that there is bias against pupils from public schools. Oxford and Cambridge are adamant this is not the case and statistics show that students from the state and independent sectors are approximately equal.

Nevertheless, in order to encourage state school pupils, a bursary of £1,000 in the first year and £500 afterwards is offered to all EU students whose family income means that they are exempt from fees.

The application process to Oxbridge is stressful, time-consuming and labour intensive. We only encourage candidates of the highest intellectual calibre to apply. Unrealistic applications lead only to inevitable rejection and disappointment. Often, application to Oxbridge is driven by the pupils' parents, particularly in the independent sector. Teachers know the pupils and it is they, in discussion with the pupils, who should make the assessment of whether the pupil is suitable for Oxbridge. Those pupils who are interested in applying but whose academic qualifications are weaker than Oxbridge expect, might be better served applying after their A levels. At that point their final A2 grades will be known, resolving any questions of their academic fitness to go to Oxbridge. Furthermore, the added year's maturity may also enhance their application.

Please note that applications for choral or music scholarships are equally competitive and the same academic standards are applied to those candidates.

## COMPLETING THE REST OF THE UCAS FORM
### When and how do I start to fill in the UCAS form?
You can start the application process from 1 September of Year 13 or in the year before you hope to begin the course. This also applies if you intend to defer access.

You can access UCAS Apply at www.ucas.com. If you are an applicant applying from a school or college, you will need to find out your unique buzzword. This will allow your application to be linked with others from the same institution. If you are a private applicant, not attached to a college or school, then this does not apply.

## Do I need to complete my application all at once?

No – indeed, this is one great advantage of UCAS Apply. Not only can you access it worldwide: you can also save it and return to it until you are ready to 'send it to the referee'. Make sure, however, that you do save before you log out.

## What is a buzzword?

This is a unique word used by each UCAS registered institution. You need it to begin your application. Ask the relevant tutor for details.

## What if I forget my password?

Try not to! Keep it safe, in several places, when you first register. However, if you do forget it you can often have it changed by the member of staff who is the UCAS super user at your school or college. If not, telephone UCAS direct on 0871 468 0 468. The line is staffed during normal office hours.

## What address should I use?

This may sound obvious: for many of you, it simply means entering your home address. If you are resident abroad for part of the year, you could enter your UK postal address, as long as someone is there to collect and open important mail on your behalf. However, you do need to be aware of the rules regarding claiming to be a UK or EU student before entering a UK address. If you are a boarder, my advice is to use your home address rather than school address. Many universities now contact you via email too, so make sure that the email address you give them is appropriate and can be accessed from school and home.

## What is my fee code?

This will let the university know how your fees are going to be paid. Usually the correct code is 02, which means that you will be applying to the Student Loans Company Ltd (www.direct.gov.uk/studentfinance) to be assessed for the level of tuition fees that you will pay. Other fee codes may mean, for example, that you will be charged as an independent student and pay considerably more. If you are an overseas applicant from outside the EU you will not enter 02. The rules about claiming to be a UK student are complex but essentially if your parents live in the UK and pay UK tax (and have done so for three years before you start university) then you qualify as a UK student.

**Note:** if you are a boarder at a UK school but do not have a parent who lives in the UK and pays UK tax, then you do not qualify. An EU student is one who lives in a country that has EU membership. For more advice contact the international office of any major UK university.

## Do I need to enter any special educational needs (SEN) I may have?

You are obliged to answer this question but you do not have to let the university know if you are dyslexic or have another special educational need. However, there is **no** evidence that anything you declare will have any bearing on your application, unless it is directly related to your ability to complete the course. Indeed, if you do enter the information on the form the university will automatically alert the relevant welfare office. As a result they may be able to offer you extra grants to purchase equipment or one-to-one help. So my advice is to be up front and open from the start.

## What is 'occupational background' and do I need to disclose that I have been in care?

This is asked for equal opportunities purposes and refers to what job the head of your household does. The information is gathered by UCAS for statistical purposes to provide the government with a profile of the applicants. It is a contentious part of the form, which is why you have the right to decline to comment in one of the drop-down boxes. There is no clear evidence that this information is used by the universities. Indeed, all the admissions tutors I spoke to when updating this book said they never even read it!

## How many choices can I make?

You can apply for up to five non-medical courses. This includes more than one course at any institution, as long as the two courses are considered properly in the Personal Statement. For instance, you could apply to read English, and English and media, at the same university in the same application cycle.

You cannot, however, apply to more than one course at either Oxford or Cambridge and you cannot apply to both in the same application cycle. You can only apply for four medicine, dentistry, veterinary medicine or veterinary science courses in one application cycle. However, you are at liberty to apply to a fifth course that is science based as a possible fall-back. A popular choice for potential medics is biomedical science.

You do not have to enter all five choices, but you ought to try at least four. Also – to demolish this myth once and for all – the choices are not in order of preference. The computer puts them in alphabetical order.

### Do the other universities know where I have applied?

No. The university only knows that you have applied to their institution and therefore cannot discriminate against you in any way.

### How do I enter my qualifications?

Remember to include all of your qualifications (GCSEs, IGCSEs, AS levels, AVCE, BTEC, A2s or IB grades). If you have a pass grade please include it. For subjects that you are still studying, give the date when you expect your exam results, in most cases August, and leave the grade pending. For GCSE double awards, click on 'GCSE double award' from the options list. Include all exams for which you have a grade, even if you have retaken them, especially Maths and English GCSE.

International students can enter their grades too. UK university admissions tutors are used to receiving applications from overseas students and know how to equate them with UK qualifications.

### What if I do not know my exam centre number?

The exam centre number should be on your exam certificates. If in doubt, ask advice from a tutor in your school or college.

### Is my employment information relevant?

In practice this is only relevant if you are a mature student with a history of full-time employment. By all means mention your summer employment history but it is unlikely to have any bearing on most applicants' success.

## How do I enter my Personal Statement?

You should write your Personal Statement in a Word document, spell-check it, then copy and paste it on to your Apply form. Statements should be approximately 550 words (4,000 characters including spaces) and in font size 12. Personal Statements must be proofread by an appropriate third party to make sure that they meet the requirements of the course. Needless to say, they must be free from spelling, punctuation and grammatical error.

## What do I do when I have completed my form?

Ensure that you have completed all sections. You will see red ticks on page 1; if there are green dots in any section box, then the box remains incomplete. Print your form off and check it for accuracy. Once your school or college tutors have agreed that your form is correct, return to your form, click that it is complete, pay the fee, answer the final security questions and send it to the referee. You cannot make any further changes after this point, unless the UCAS super user intervenes on your behalf.

## How do I pay?

This depends on your own circumstances. Some students pay the school direct, which then pays on your behalf. However, the majority will now pay either by credit or debit card.

## What happens next?

Your school or college will normally check your form thoroughly, especially your academic results. An academic reference is attached and the form is then sent to UCAS.

On receipt of your form, UCAS send you confirmation, your application number and your password for tracking your application through the UCAS Track system. Please keep this information safe.

Your form is then sent electronically to your universities. You receive replies either directly from the university and UCAS, or just from UCAS. Only offers communicated through UCAS are valid. Note: it can take months for your university to reply. You should have heard from them all by early April.

**Communications with UCAS:** you are asked whether you want to receive information by telephone (mobile), text message or email. If you have indicated that you are happy to receive information by any or all of these means, please ensure that your contact details are up to date and that emails from UCAS will not be picked up by your spam email filter.

The UCAS hotline number for applicants, open for office hours during the working week, is +44 (0)871 468 0 468.

## How do I reply to offers?

In short, you reply via the online tracking system. It will not allow you to choose your first choice (CF) or second choice (CI) until all your universities have responded. This can be frustrating, but be patient.

PART TWO
# ACADEMIC PROFILES

# ACCOUNTING

This profile was written using information provided by an admissions tutor at the University of Essex. The information in this profile is useful to all applicants, but some of the advice is pertinent to Essex in particular.

## SUBJECT OVERVIEW

Financial information plays an important role in society because of its centrality in decision-making in a variety of organisations. For example, financial information is vital in decisions such as:

- what effect will an increase in the price of a company's products have on its profitability?
- will it be beneficial for a company to change its method of production?
- what will be the effect of a reduction in the funding of local government on the level of services that can be provided?
- how much additional funding does a hospital need to substantially decrease its waiting lists?

Accounting courses tend to focus both on the techniques used in accounting and the critique and evaluation of current accounting practices. Accounting degrees also cover other issues such as the appropriateness of information disclosed to shareholders, the effectiveness of regulation of auditing and the economic consequences of a change in accounting policy. Depending on the degree you study, you may also have the opportunity to study finance, management and economics.

# WHAT SKILLS OR ATTRIBUTES DO ADMISSIONS TUTORS LOOK FOR IN A GOOD APPLICANT?

Applicants need to show a strong aptitude and enthusiasm for business in general, and accounting specifically. A good applicant would also be able to show an awareness of accounting and its impact in the wider world, through keeping informed of current affairs and developments in the business world and an awareness of the relationship between private and public companies and the government and regulatory bodies.

Academically, students should demonstrate ability in mathematics, although the need for A level Maths may vary among institutions. Applicants for accounting may also be studying courses in accounting, business and economics, although these subjects are not usually compulsory entry requirements. Non-academic traits beneficial to an accounting applicant would be demonstration of an eye for detail, experience of working in a team, good communication and potential leadership skills.

# WHAT DOES A GOOD PERSONAL STATEMENT LOOK LIKE?

Students should clearly state why they have chosen to study accounting and what first sparked their interest in the subject. An awareness of accountancy as a career is advantageous, so any students with work experience should highlight this. It is useful to explain what the work experience involved and why it led them to choose to apply for accounting at university.

Students could also mention their current subjects studied at school OR college which are relevant to the course. This is especially important if a student's current studies have inspired their choice of degree. Their current studies may also have provided skills which will be useful at university level, such as analytical skills, business knowledge and critical thinking. An awareness and understanding of current business and accounting issues is also useful to demonstrate, as is any knowledge of business practices picked up through part-time employment.

# Examples of a good Personal Statement

Accounting is an analytical interpretation of money; I see accounting as the backbone of every organisation be it large or small. It decides the success or failure of a business and it adds and recognises the value of money. Without accounting money will be of little or no value. My passion for business and inquisitiveness about the current financial crisis have cemented my decision to study for a degree in accounting.

✓ This opening paragraph shows a clear interest and enthusiasm for accounting both as a degree and as a career choice. It is important to explain your interest in your chosen subject in the opening lines of the Personal Statement.

My interest in accounting started three years ago when I began working part time as a bookkeeper in a family business. I helped with collecting and processing invoices, made entries of debit and credit in a book and I was further involved in making stock orders and arranging them in their respective storage places. I have also worked in a restaurant where I was responsible for making sure the sales book was balanced.

✓ First-hand experience of accounting in part-time employment or work experience is useful to highlight.

While studying A level Accounting in college I have developed a strong interest within the subject and would like to improve my knowledge by continuing to study the subject at university. By studying accounts in college, I learnt a lot about how accounting is used in a variety of business situations and the measurement of financial transactions. I am also studying A level Economics, which helps me with my accounts as the subjects combine well. By studying both these subjects, I have a greater understanding of the various concepts, methods and analytical skills involved in them.

✓ An effective way of describing how A level study has strengthened the applicant's interest and prepared the applicant for accounting at university level.

To broaden my understanding and knowledge, I have been reading The Economist and The Financial Times newspapers. This gives me an insight into the state of economy and business organisations and allows me to be up to date with information that happens in the economy. Currently, global financial markets have been undergoing serious problems, causing the UK's economy to suffer a serious downturn. I believe accounting links in well with economics, as it allows me to convert a true and fair picture of the business world, which will therefore help me to enhance my accounting knowledge.

✓ It is always a good idea to refer to current affairs as awareness of business in the wider world can be an advantage.

> During my time at sixth form, I have developed many new skills and improved those I already have. I have become more organised, designating periods for study and meeting coursework deadlines. A key skill for an accountant is to be comfortable with working with figures and numbers. I have been in the top sets for maths and have become extremely confident in dealing with formulas and numbers. The fundamental skill, in which I have developed, is becoming more independent in  researching and teaching new skills.

✓ Highlighting skills learned at school/college and applying them to university study, and the course specifically, shows thoughtfulness and some awareness of the applicant's motivation for university study.

## Examples of a poor Personal Statement

> I have always known that maths was going to be what I wanted to focus on throughout school. It is my favourite subject and I look upon it with an optimistic view when I am confronted with a challenging problem. I enjoy applying different skills to help myself find the answer that I am looking for, and always feel I have done something important when I see what I have tried is correct. I would love a career that would apply my interest in mathematics.

✗ On reading this opening paragraph, admissions tutors would probably wonder why this candidate is applying for accounting.

> I am a hard working and enthusiastic student. I have good communication and people skills. I am well organised and have strong analytical skills. I also have very strong numeracy and literacy skills and enjoy working under pressure.

✗ Simply describing your skills is not enough – it is preferable to give examples and explain how your personal skills have developed.

> I have identified your university as one which offers the course best suited to my needs. My ambition is to be an accountant and I believe the course I am applying for will allow me to get the qualification I need to go into a career.

✗ This was a final paragraph and the first reference to accounting in the Personal Statement. The subject choice should comprise the majority of a Personal Statement's content.

My thirst for knowledge will be quenched if given an opportunity to study this course in your university which I have such passion for. I'm looking forward to gaining status as a chartered accountant and feel ready to confidently tackle the challenges that this career will throw at me.

✗ Try not to get caught up in clumsy language which has little meaning.

 **TOP TIPS**

**1** Show a knowledge of accountancy as a career as well as a subject choice

**2** Mention and give details about any work experience or part-time employment that may enhance your application

**3** Highlight skills you have which will be useful when studying the degree: numerical skills, team working, commitment and organisational skills

**4** Show an interest in accountancy and business which exists beyond the classroom

**5** Show that you are looking forward to studying this course at degree level and to the university experience

 **THINGS TO AVOID**

**1** Simply stating your interests without any further explanation

**2** Saying you want to be an accountant because a friend or family member is an accountant: this is not a good enough reason by itself

**3** Poor spelling, punctuation and grammar: the way you present your work is just as important as the content

**4** Making sweeping statements referring to 'heart's desires' and 'great passions'. It is more effective to be subtle in your enthusiasm

**5** Focusing your interests purely on business or maths; if this is where your interests really lie, you should consider a joint degree!

#  RECOMMENDED READING AND WEBSITES

- Jenny Keaveney, *Careers Uncovered: Accountancy*, Trotman Publishing, 2010
- A Britton and C Waterston (2009), *Financial Accounting*, 5th edition, FT Prentice Hall: A useful introductory accounting textbook
- The professional accounting bodies have informative websites which contain topical information on accounting issues. Examples are the sites of the Institute of Chartered Accountants in England and Wales (www.icaew.com) and the Association of Chartered Certified Accountants: (www.accaglobal.com)
- Finally, if you think you might want to train with a large firm of chartered accountants, look at the website of Deloitte as an example: www.deloitte.co.uk

# AMERICAN STUDIES

**This academic profile was written using information provided by an admissions tutor from Swansea University. The information in this profile is useful to all applicants, but please be aware that some of the advice is pertinent to that department in particular.**

 ## SUBJECT OVERVIEW

As the last global superpower, the USA has an immediate and continuing impact on all our lives. It influences our culture, our economy, and our political outlook. Its foreign policy affects our future. To know and understand the nature of America, its art, culture, historical and political traditions, is to appreciate more fully the real forces driving the 21st century.

American studies is for students with a broad-based interest in American life and American culture, especially for those with a particular interest in American history, literature, politics, film or popular culture. It is also for students who would relish the opportunity to try out many different approaches (from film analysis to exploring the American landscape), develop new skills (such as decoding advertisements or studying historical documents) and explore many disciplines, which can also include art, music, communications and sociology alongside the core components of history, literature and politics and film.

American studies can also be for those who would like to experience American life first-hand, with the opportunities to study four-year degrees at a number of higher education institutions and spend a whole year studying, travelling and exploring the USA. Students who choose a three-year degree are likely to have the experience of being taught by professors from the USA and could have the option of spending a semester studying in the USA depending on the course.

# WHAT SKILLS OR ATTRIBUTES DO ADMISSIONS TUTORS LOOK FOR IN A GOOD APPLICANT?

American studies does not assume any prior study of American culture, but does assume that prospective students are interested in current affairs, are willing to engage with all aspects of American culture from gangsta rap to Hollywood blockbusters to *The Great Gatsby*, and are flexible and open-minded enough to cope with a wide range of teaching styles, methodological approaches and source material – whether presidential speeches, classic American novels or letters and memoirs from the American Civil War. Although most prospective students will have studied English, history, media or politics at A level, the nature of American studies is such that most departments will be more than willing to look at any candidate who possesses a real drive and enthusiastic commitment to studying the USA. Grade requirements vary, but on average you could expect to be asked to gain between ABB and BBC (or equivalent).

# WHAT DOES A GOOD PERSONAL STATEMENT LOOK LIKE?

The most important thing to demonstrate when applying to American studies is a broad commitment to studying all aspects of American life and letters. Be as specific as you can – talk about American films you have enjoyed, American writers you are interested in, cover which aspects of American history (there's more of it than you might think!) especially excite you. You should also signal that you are aware of, and actively engaged with, contemporary issues – whether the presidential election, events in Iraq, or all sorts of other global issues. American studies is a 'transnational' discipline, in that it also explores the impact of American policies and products on the rest of the world – so you could also talk about issues of globalisation, foreign policy, or the relationship between America and the UK.

Stress your flexibility and willingness to try new things – American studies requires a great deal of energy and adaptability as it covers so many different areas. If you have been to the US, talk about your experience – even if it was only a family trip to Orlando, you can still touch upon what aspects of America you found familiar and any parts of American life which felt to you to be strangely 'foreign'. Talk about your interests and activities in a passionate and committed manner – we are looking for well-rounded individuals with a keen interest in a wide variety of fields.

## Example of a good Personal Statement

> America is the most powerful and influential country in the world, as the phrase 'When America sneezes we all catch a cold' suggests.

✓ A good opening quote, and a clear understanding of the importance of the topic.

> I found studying Martin Luther King and civil rights at A level very interesting as well as America and the Vietnam War.

✓ Specific examples really add critical weight to the statement and give an indication of the areas that the candidate is already interested in.

> I have developed a further interest after visiting family in Arizona and experiencing first-hand the culture of America.

✓ While first-hand knowledge of America is not necessary, it does provide a basis for why the candidate might want to learn more.

> I want to read American studies because I believe I will find it both interesting and fascinating.

✓ Enthusiasm and energy are key factors.

> I am interested in studying how the global superpower influences the culture, economy and political outlook in my daily life, United Kingdom, and the rest of the world.

✓ Suggests an awareness of, and interest in, global events and current affairs.

> I also feel it will further the skills and knowledge that I have already started building on in A levels. Not only have I learnt about America and some of its stages in history through college, but also due to my enjoyment of reading, I have read about it in books such as Little Women and The Big Sleep.

✓ The candidate covers both history and literature and strengthens their application by including specific titles and examples. A love of reading is very, very important!

> The subjects I have chosen for A levels are English language, sociology and history. These subjects have helped to provide skills such as time organisation and structured writing.

✓ Shows a clear understanding of the study skills required.

> They have also provided me with different ways in which to see the world, sociology showing the structure of society and the way people can act. In studying America it will be interesting to see the culture and society of another country and how it can change and develop. This will enable me to expand my views by challenging preconceived ideas to see whether they are right or wrong.

✓ The candidate understands that university education is about acquiring the skills to argue, discuss and debate.

> I have found studying history to be stimulating and challenging and it has helped me learn how to construct my ideas and arguments through assignments and essays. This has also helped me to develop analytical and evaluating skills which will be a great asset when studying American studies. I'm looking forward to developing a greater depth of understanding of the world's largestsuperpower.

✓ A confident, well-written and critically focused conclusion.

This is an example of a very good Personal Statement. The candidate sets forward their reasons for undertaking the course, and demonstrates a real sense of commitment and academic drive. They also provide a number of specific examples of areas of American culture they have already found to be stimulating and provocative, choosing these from the central areas of both history (Vietnam, civil rights) and literature (*Little Women* and *The Big Sleep*). The candidate suggests in a clear and intelligent manner how the analytical skills they have already acquired will be of enormous relevance to their chosen degree scheme.

They also demonstrate a lucid understanding of what the subject is, and the degree to which it matches their own interests and enthusiasms. The stress on the relationship between the USA and the UK, and indeed, America and the rest of the world also suggests an awareness of global issues and the importance of studying the basis and nature of American power and influence.

## Example of a poor Personal Statement

> The current judicial system is far from perfect, but being able to change the views of people and help in the struggle for equality is very important to me.

✗ This seems both very vague and not really relevant to American studies – has the student applied to the right degree scheme?

> I feel that this is the perfect time to study with my good educational background and combination of business and general studies.

✗ How does this relate to American studies? The candidate doesn't seem to be aware of the different elements that make up the scheme.

> Although I took my A levels in August 2006, I never thought about university, as I didn't think it was for me. However, after nearly two years working for a telematic company I have become disillusioned in the workplace and can't imagine doing this line of work for the rest of my life, as I would like to make a difference. This is where applying for university comes in and gaining a degree as I strive for excellence.

✗ This seems very negative, as if the candidate is simply looking to escape the mundane nature of their current employment. Where is the commitment, the energy, or the imaginative enthusiasm? It is also a very badly constructed sentence.

> I am an independent, responsible and confident person who strives for perfection.

✗ Too vague – we need specific examples here.

> I can communicate with others who may find it difficult to do so. I can work independently and in a group, I can carry out tasks with the minimum of help.

✗ The candidate needs to stress their critical and analytical skills rather than specifically work-related ones.

> My hobbies include playing football, tennis, and anything sports-related. As I love challenging myself and trying to become the best I possibly can in whatever activity I am pursuing.

✗ The second sentence isn't a sentence – this gives the impression that the candidate is slipshod and puts very little effort into what they do.

This candidate makes no mention of American studies whatsoever; rather the distinct suspicion is that the candidate, unsure of where to go next, has applied to a wide range of courses (presumably including law or criminology) and has simply written a general and very sloppy Personal Statement. They fail to demonstrate any awareness of the degree scheme to which they are notionally applying, and the statement is particularly lacking in any concrete examples of why they would want to undertake American studies, or which aspects of the course (for example, film or history) they would find most interesting. The general tone is negative and unfocused; it feels as if the candidate is trapped in a dead-end job and will do anything to get out. Finally, as an individual who states that they strive for excellence, there are far too many errors in the piece – this gives the impression that the statement was cobbled together with very little thought or forward planning.

 **TOP TIPS**

**1** Be enthusiastic: you can do anything with your life right now – what drives you to choose American studies? Make this clear in your statement

 **THINGS TO AVOID**

**1** Writing your application as if you simply want to visit the USA as a tourist! American studies is a challenging and academically rigorous degree scheme

**2** Be relevant: gear your reference to specific aspects of politics, literature, history or film

**3** Name names: who are your favourite writers or film-makers, what history books have you read (and by whom?)

**4** Assert your individuality: American studies allows you to mould the degree scheme around your own interests and ideas, so say what these are!

**5** Be aware: of the news, of global events, of the economic and cultural forces that are all around us

**6** Be specific: while joint honours students will want to discuss both aspects of their degree, it is important that you stress why you're specifically interested in American studies

**2** Silly errors, haphazard grammar, and badly organised sentences: you will be spending a great deal of your time writing essays, so indicate that you possess the necessary skills

**3** Oversimplifications, clichés and pat answers: a university degree is all about discussion, argument and debate

**4** Getting names or book titles wrong: you should name names and be specific – but make sure that you get all the names or titles of books right in the first place!

## RECOMMENDED READING AND WEBSITES

- Read American novels, historical works and quality newspapers for current affairs in the USA
- American Studies Centre: www.americansc.org.uk
- British Association for American Studies:www.baas.ac.uk

I am grateful for the support of Swansea University (www.swan.ac.uk/american) in the preparation of this profile. Other highly rated courses include those at the universities Warwick, Manchester, Liverpool, UEA and Lancaster.

# ARCHAEOLOGY AND ANTHROPOLOGY

This academic profile was written using information provided by admissions tutors at Southampton University and focuses on archaeology as a single honours discipline. The information in this profile is useful to all applicants, but please be aware that some of the advice is pertinent to that department in particular.

## SUBJECT OVERVIEW

Archaeology is a subject that provides the opportunity to uncover past peoples and their worlds. From their material remains, you can find out about their daily lives: what they ate, what they wore and the kinds of landscapes they lived in. You can also find out about the 'big questions' about how society was organised, the scale of trade and exchange, belief structures and technology. Archaeology offers a unique blend of humanities and science, practical and theoretical. For this reason it offers excellent transferable skills which mean graduates can go into many careers.

## WHAT SKILLS OR ATTRIBUTES DO ADMISSIONS TUTORS LOOK FOR IN A GOOD APPLICANT?

Archaeology A level is still taught by only a small number of colleges, so we do not have any specific subject requirements, and our students come from a diversity of paths: either all sciences, all arts, or a combination. For archaeological science and combined honours programmes, we do look for a good grade in specific appropriate subjects, and this would be true of most other departments. That being said, students who do study archaeology to A level would need to highlight what aspects of their work they have found most interesting and discuss their fieldwork opportunities and coursework plans.

More important is that you should be able to demonstrate an interest in finding out about the past, whether from excavation or museum experience, or from family holidays visiting British castles, or the ruins of Pompeii. We look for a questioning mind and enthusiasm, as evidenced by a good academic track record at A level and GCSE, and performance at interview.

As archaeology is largely about teamwork, we also look for ability to work as part of a team: you do not have to be the life and soul of the party, but you do need to be willing to participate and join in.

# WHAT DOES A GOOD PERSONAL STATEMENT LOOK LIKE?

You should use your Personal Statement as an opportunity to show why you are interested in the study of the past. Only approximately 25% of applicants will have studied archaeology at AS or A2 level, so why do you want to study it at university? What stirred your interest – was it a childhood visit to an ancient monument, or a particular TV programme? What have you done to further that interest – visiting more sites in Britain and abroad, reading specific books, taking part on an excavation, or work experience in a museum? What skills do you have from your GCSEs and A levels, or from extracurricular activities, that prepare you for an archaeology degree? If you are applying for a combined honours degree, why do you want to do that particular combination?

## TOP TIPS

**1** Say what it is that excites you about the past

**2** Mention specific sites and museums you have visited

**3** If you are applying for a combined honours degree, say why you want to study both subjects together

**4** If you have an interest in a

##  THINGS TO AVOID

**1** Plagiarising your statement by downloading it from the web or copying it word for word from a book

**2** Applying for combined honours in archaeology and history, and then only talking about how interested you are in history and failing to mention archaeology: tutors will assume particular aspect of archaeology: for example, Romans or animal bones – mention it

**5** Be positive

**6** Make sure that you present yourself in as compelling and interesting way as you can

you will not get the grades for a history degree and are using the combined honours as a back door into the single honours

**3** Spelling and grammatical mistakes in your Personal Statements

**4** Saying anything about yourself which is not true: you're usually found out at interview

**5** Including left-field archaeological ideas: the Pyramids were not built by aliens!

---

##  RECOMMENDED READING AND WEBSITES

- Council for British Archaeology: www.britarch.ac.uk
- *Current Archaeology*: www.archaeology.co.uk

I am grateful for the support of Southampton University (www.arch.soton.ac.uk) in the preparation of this profile. Other highly rated courses include those at the universities of Durham, York, Sheffield, Cambridge and Oxford.

# BIOLOGICAL SCIENCES

**This profile was written using information provided by an admissions tutor at the University of Essex. The information in this profile is useful to all applicants, but some of the advice is pertinent to Essex in particular.**

##  SUBJECT OVERVIEW

Biological sciences is a broad-based degree course which can cover many topics ranging from cell and molecular biology, to genetics, marine and freshwater biology, biodiversity and applied ecology. Most biological sciences degrees will provide a broad and balanced knowledge of modern biology, centred on the organism but including molecular, genetic, cellular and population aspects, and the opportunity to specialise in particular areas. Biological sciences courses will cover field and laboratory skills and training in scientific methods as well as theoretical knowledge.

## WHAT SKILLS OR ATTRIBUTES DO ADMISSIONS TUTORS LOOK FOR IN A GOOD APPLICANT?

Applicants should be able to demonstrate a firm knowledge and serious interest in biology and issues related to the subject such as stem cell therapy, vaccines, conservation, evolution and climate change. As biological sciences is such a large area of study which covers many topics, universities tend to offer the opportunity to specialise within the course. Therefore if an applicant can express an interest in a certain area of biology, this can be advantageous (but make sure the institutions you are applying to offer the specialism you are looking for!). Most biological sciences courses will require previous study of biology to A level standard or equivalent.

## WHAT DOES A GOOD PERSONAL STATEMENT LOOK LIKE?

### Examples of a good Personal Statement

I have always enjoyed biology so it was a natural A level choice for me. I have enjoyed all the topics we have covered, but particularly the body's response to infection, bacteria and viruses such as TB and HIV and also the complex way in which these foreign organisms become antibiotic resistant. My other A level subjects of geography and psychology have contributed to my interest greatly. Our geography field trip to France opened my eyes to different ecological phenomena, especially the rare plant life in the peat bogs of Mont Lozere. In psychology, I found the research into mental disorders such as schizophrenia and depression particularly interesting. This has increased my desire to find out more about these disorders and why they develop and the involvement of the brain from a biological point of view.

✓ Discussing your current studies and how they have sparked your interest will help explain your interest in the subject and why you have chosen it at degree level.

Within biological sciences I have a keen enthusiasm for microbiology. Studying viruses is of a particular interest to me as they are so prominent in the lives of humans and yet we know little about them. I am also fascinated by the way in which bacteria can mutate to create resistances to dangers and reproduce exponentially. Both biology and chemistry have fuelled and moulded my interest in microbiology. They have given me a greater understanding of the chemical processes that occur in the world from the reason why ice floats to the production of aspirin. It is for these reasons that I wish to study biological sciences at university.

✓ It is useful to explain your interest in a sub-section of biology and why certain areas appeal to you.

Last year I organised a placement at the Royal London Hospital in the Oral Pathology department. I was able to see cut-up biopsy specimens from the neck and mouth. This was particularly exciting to see in the larger specimens where it was vital to locate the small lymph nodes. Seeing the diagnostic process applied to many different cases allowed me to appreciate the importance of histology. I would love to be involved in this type of work since the job was challenging, involving much investigative practical work, and important as patients relied on the results and diagnosis.

Recently I spent a week in Wales on an ecology field trip studying the growth rate of Ascophyllum nodosum. I greatly enjoyed being able to experience the process first hand, forming my own data and following the investigation from start to finish.

✓ It is useful to discuss any relevant practical experience you have had and what you learned or discovered from it, whether it furthered your academic knowledge and/or confirmed your career plans.

In my spare time I like to engage in football and basketball and also attend the gym as keeping fit is important to me. I use my knowledge of the skeletal muscles from biology by applying it to my gym sessions in order to get the best out of my workouts.

✓ Referring to biology in your extracurricular activities can be an effective way of proving your interest in the subject.

> I understand that university life will be very challenging, but I am confident that it will give me the best chance to achieve my potential and enable me to contribute to a greater understanding of biology and biological processes. I also hope that it will lead the way forward to a successful career in this field.

✓ It is useful to summarise the content of your Personal Statement in a closing paragraph.

## Examples of a poor Personal Statement

> I regularly buy the New Scientist magazine and the National Geographic to catch up on any news in the world of science.

✗ Simply stating that you have these magazines without any further discussion of what you have read does not provide us with much information about your interest in the subject.

> I have researched and thought thoroughly about the type of course I would like to undertake. I want to now pursue different areas in my life and I think that marine studies is a good choice because it is something that interests me as well as providing me with new knowledge, new skills and giving me the opportunity to use my existing academic skills. I feel that this will give me a new challenge but also give me the chance to do something I have always wanted to do with an end result of gaining one of my aims in life.

✗ This paragraph is quite vague with little detail on **why** marine studies is of interest to the applicant.

> I formerly worked in a care home but I found the work very difficult emotionally so I resigned.

✗ It is advisable to focus on the positive aspects of your part-time or voluntary work rather than bring up negative experiences. In addition, information about current jobs or work placements is more relevant to your application than former ones.

> My ambition is to participate in conservation abroad. I feel that the knowledge and experience I will gain from the course will enable me to achieve this ambition.

✗ Again this paragraph lacks detail – it is always better to be analytical rather than descriptive in your Personal Statement.

> Although the long-term future of the planet may seem bleak, I wish to play my part in protecting, preserving and conserving it so that we try to preserve it for future generations.

✗ Once again, it is not a good idea to be negative!

**TOP TIPS**

**1** Display a strong enthusiasm for biology and explain why the subject interests you

**2** Provide details about the courses you are currently studying and skills and knowledge which will help you in higher education

**3** Show an interest in specialising during your degree

**4** Discuss any practical experience you have had, such as work experience or field trips

**5** If your extracurricular activities or hobbies are at all relevant to biology, do highlight this. Otherwise, highlight the transferable skills you have gained from these activities

 **THINGS TO AVOID**

**1** Simply stating your interests without any further explanation

**2** Being negative in any part of your Personal Statement creates an overall negative impression of you: always be positive!

**3** Describing your activities, hobbies and interests but not giving any further details about them or what you have gained from them

**4** Neglecting to talk about biological sciences or why it interests you: this is the most important information!

**5** Showing a lack of understanding or awareness of the impact of biology/ecology/conservation etc. in the outside world

 **RECOMMENDED READING AND WEBSITES**

- Biochemical Society: www.biochemsoc.org
- British Ecological Society: www.britishecologicalsociety.org/
- University of Essex Biological Sciences: www.essex.ac.uk/bs
- The Royal Society: http://royalsociety.org – follow the Science Issues link
- Society of Biology, for links to careers advice: www.societyofbiology.org

I am grateful to the University of Essex for their help in preparing this profile. Other highly rated courses can be found at the universities of Cambridge, York, Oxford, Leicester and St Andrew's.

# BUSINESS, BANKING, MANAGEMENT AND ACTUARIAL SCIENCE

This academic profile is a composite of information provided by admissions tutors at both Aston University and City University. The information is useful to all applicants, but some of the advice is pertinent to Aston or City in particular.

 ## SUBJECT OVERVIEW

The practice of business and management (and all the other specialisms, such as accounting, marketing and economics) is a varied and fascinating subject and taking place around us every day. The globalised business and financial world and power of brands, finance, marketing, consumer behaviour, large organisations and multinationals, along with the importance of entrepreneurship and forward thinking, means a business degree is useful in many careers. Many business degrees include a fantastic opportunity to take a placement year in industry or work or study abroad as part of the course. Business students are a massively varied group of people, often from all over the world, offering lots of new perspectives, friends and future contacts.

Business studies and management are essentially practice-orientated subjects that focus on the organisation and its operations. Business studies analyses the key functions that most organisations need to develop in order to survive and prosper, whether commercial, not for profit or public agencies. It includes a diverse range of subjects which have developed a range of theories and models, requiring differing techniques and skills. Management is both a practical skill and a body of theory that draws on a multitude of thinkers who have written on a wide range of aspects of the subject over the last two centuries.

Banking and finance is the study of the financial markets and the role of banking within that. The recent turmoil in these markets underlines the enormous importance of this sector to a modern economy. The subject focuses on different types of financial markets, institutions and their roles, as well as security analysis and valuation. Change is a feature of the subject in response to evolving market conditions and theory development by academic and practitioner researchers. Models and theories tend to be quantitative. Students would be expected to handle the applications of these models. As such, a minimum of an AS level in Maths would be a requirement of most courses.

The actuarial science degree prepares students for a career as an actuary or any other area involving finance and risk. Actuaries are employed to assess risks in a variety of business situations and advise their clients or employers as to the likely costs associated with the various possible outcomes. Probability and statistics are at the heart of their professional expertise. Students will learn to use and apply the relevant mathematical models, probability and statistical theory and information technology. Communication skills are also prized by the actuarial profession.

# WHAT SKILLS OR ATTRIBUTES DO ADMISSIONS TUTORS LOOK FOR IN A GOOD APPLICANT?

All degrees require good numeracy, literacy and reasoning skills.

We need to see evidence of commitment to a business and management degree, for instance a demonstrable interest in the business world. A good candidate would have an awareness of recent issues in the UK economy that are relevant, for instance the recent upheaval in the sub-prime market and its impact on banking and finance. Academic skills might be illustrated by a Business Studies or Economics A level or equivalent, but this is not always obligatory.

Maths is another skill that is relevant, although the need for an A level will vary from course to course. A good candidate will show an awareness of globalisation, customer focus, organisations and how they work, the importance of brands and marketing, finance and economics. A candidate interested in banking and finance would need to put forward a case as to why they want to specialise at this stage. No reason not to, but this ambition needs to be explained – 'to make money' is not a good response! Particular awareness of the current banking crisis and its impact on the world economy would be expected in a statement.

Non-academic skills might include good communication and teamwork skills, evidence of leadership or putting forward new ideas – for example part-time or voluntary work. Initiative is rewarded, so show evidence of projects you have initiated such as student magazines or student-led fundraising schemes. The Young Enterprise and Duke of Edinburgh's Award schemes are other means of showing these attributes.

Actuarial science requires a high level of mathematical knowledge on entry (A at A level or equivalent). Those who have good A level scores in other subjects but have failed to get the requisite mathematical score are directed to an additional one-year pre-university foundation course to bring their mathematical skills up to an acceptable level. Students who do well on the actuarial science degree are those with a genuine passion for mathematics and who enjoy applying their mathematical skills to solving real-world problems. Students also need an interest in the financial world. The actuarial science degree is demanding and so students who are well organised and self-motivated are also well placed to succeed.

---

## WHAT DOES A GOOD PERSONAL STATEMENT LOOK LIKE?

Your Personal Statement is a key part of your UCAS application form. Most good business schools in the UK receive a lot of applications, many of which are from applicants who meet or are predicted to meet our academic entry requirements, so it is essential that you write a good Personal Statement in order to stand out from the competition.

Make it clear and concise. Clearly state why you want to study business, management or another related course. Make it clear what your interests are and your specific subjects at school or college – for example, business, accounting, geography, economics – which you feel are relevant and worth talking about. Emphasise the relevant skills you have learnt and the books, newspapers and magazines that you have read to extend your understanding of the subject. You can see good examples below. You are encouraged to refer to demonstrable interests you might have in the business world. In this regard the Young Enterprise scheme and other similar schemes are useful. Reference to current issues affecting business is always welcome.

Admissions officers realise that many applicants will also apply to other institutions and may still be making up their mind between a couple of subjects. You will not therefore be disadvantaged if your Personal Statement states that you are interested in studying BSc Management or another discipline such as sociology. As long as you then explain what it is about those two very different courses that appeals to you, this will not be held against you.

Finally, in order to optimise your chance of being offered a place, the best piece of advice we can give you is to submit a neat and complete application. A Personal Statement with several spelling or grammatical errors does not engender much confidence in your writing skills. Competition is very high at top schools, so do not undermine your chances with lazy spelling or poor grammar. Ask a parent or teacher to proofread it carefully.

 **TOP TIPS**

**1** Emphasise the skills that you have already acquired that are both academic and non-academic

**2** Mention any work experience, business experience and/or taster courses that you have attended that may enhance your application

**3** Read prospectuses and websites: business courses are different across the UK in how and what they teach and specialise in, and in how you are assessed. Your understanding of these needs to be reflected in your Personal Statements

 **THINGS TO AVOID**

**1** Repetition

**2** Unsubstantiated claims that you could not defend in an interview

**3** Poor spelling, punctuation and grammar: check and read it carefully. You would be surprised how many errors we see that are the result of lazy proofreading or reliance on spell checkers

**4** Sweeping generalisations such as 'I have always been passionate about a career in . . .': this is rarely true!

**4** Do your research in plenty of time during March to July of Year 12 or equivalent: be ready to complete and send off your UCAS form well before Christmas in Year 13 or equivalent. Early research also helps to establish enough time to prepare your statement properly

**5** Choosing a university or particular course just because it is high in the league tables or your parents/teachers think it makes them look good: choose a university because you think the course content, reputation, graduate employability, teaching and social facilities are right for you. If appropriate, you might indicate that you have done this in the body of your statement. Do not mention individual universities, but do indicate in general terms that you have done your research

**6** Assuming admissions tutors know all about you: they can't check you out on Facebook or YouTube – all they have is the UCAS form. So use it to sell yourself!

**7** Using humour or crass statements on your Personal Statement: keep it concise, serious and realistic but positive

# RECOMMENDED READING AND WEBSITES

- Philip Coggan, *The Money Machine: How the City Works*, Penguin, 2009 – a great introductory read for those interested in finance and banking
- Business/finance pages of papers such as the *Guardian, The Times*, the *Independent* and the *Daily Telegraph* to get a range of perspectives
- *The Economist* (www.economist.com): web version of the weekly newspaper – lots of political economy, with a libertarian slant. Some articles are only available for those with subscription
- *The Financial Times* (www.ft.com): excellent source for business economics. Also contains a portfolio service for you to build your own virtual share portfolio and track your wealth
- *Marketing Week*: www.marketingweek.co.uk

- www.actuaries.org.uk – the website for the actuarial society. The starting point for anyone wanting to get into this lucrative but demanding area of business
- The Bank of England (www.bankofengland.co.uk): good source of information about macroeconomic policy in the UK, specially designed for A level students
- OneWorld.net (www.oneworld.net): source of information on world economic events, giving an alternative view to that of the World Bank and International Monetary Fund (IMF)
- The World Bank (www.worldbank.org): a detailed starting point for information and analysis of development issues

I am grateful for the support received from Aston University (www.abs.aston.ac.uk) in the preparation of this profile. Other highly rated courses include those at the universities of Oxford, Leicester, Imperial, St Andrew's and Warwick.

# CLASSICS

## Classics, classical studies, ancient history, classical archaeology

**This academic profile was written using information provided by an admissions tutor at King's College, University of London. The information is useful to all applicants, but some of the advice is pertinent to King's College, University of London in particular.**

## SUBJECT OVERVIEW

The cultures of the ancient world, embracing everything from the palaces of Bronze Age Crete to Roman cities on the African frontier, are fascinating to study in their own right. But because classical texts and art have significantly influenced thought, literature and politics since ancient times, they also offer a skeleton key to understanding much of Western culture.

Classics, classical studies, ancient history and classical archaeology make up a family of degree programmes offering different avenues of approach to ancient cultures, via their languages and literature (in the original or in translation), their political, military and cultural history, their material remains, and their effects on later times.

Although each individual programme has its own specific focus and methods, they also offer the possibility of combining a diverse range of subjects: classicists may combine historical and archaeological courses with their work on Homer, Virgil, and tragedy; ancient historians may move between Herodotus, Hadrian's Wall and lyric poetry; and classical studies students might look at the early Iron Age alongside their Ovid. To students who have studied classical subjects at school, the university curriculum offers a new range of subjects spanning ideas, objects and areas of which they may have been completely unaware before.

A classics-related degree has the advantage of being very highly regarded by employers, while offering an unpredictable and interesting course of study. Students often travel with their subject, venturing through the modern countries of the Mediterranean, Europe and the Middle East with the eye of an informed explorer. These are the original interdisciplinary degrees, offering the opportunity to experience cutting-edge methods and approaches for historical, literary and archaeological study more generally.

## WHAT SKILLS OR ATTRIBUTES DO ADMISSIONS TUTORS LOOK FOR IN A GOOD APPLICANT?

As a good classics applicant you will have the same general skills and attributes as any good humanities applicant: enthusiasm, self-motivation, a desire to learn, an appetite both for different perspectives and for challenging questions. The King's College London admissions team hope to see applicants who enjoy independently exploring new topics, whether in the library, the museum, or the field; people who want to engage with new problems and techniques, and to get behind the clichés of mass-media versions of ancient myth and conflict. This is an approach that will be mirrored in similar departments elsewhere.

Because of their different angles of approach, the different degree programmes within classics do not all call for exactly the same skills and strengths; there are variations in emphasis from one university department to another. In particular, it is a good idea for applicants without an ancient language to check what quantity of work in classical Greek or Latin a particular programme is going to expect.

Departments that require compulsory language work from all their students want to see evidence that you have some aptitude and interest in learning languages. If you have been lucky enough to acquire ancient languages at school, bear in mind that university assessment will require more extended commentary and essay writing in all topics, so the ability to write as well as translate fluently is key.

Departments recruiting for degrees in classical archaeology will also prefer candidates with an ability to look carefully at visual evidence and to produce some ideas about how material objects may be used to reconstruct the ancient world. Admissions staff for both archaeology and ancient history will be interested in how analytically you can think about evidence and piece together your ideas based on it.

Depending on the university's balance between individual and group teaching, universities may look for evidence that you will be a responsive student, willing to voice your opinion in a group, or to discuss your ideas with the lecturer and with fellow students. Your key qualities are enthusiasm and motivation.

## WHAT DOES A GOOD PERSONAL STATEMENT LOOK LIKE?

Remember who you are talking to in your statement: the admissions tutor is a member of the academic staff whose job it is to let in students who they think will be interesting and enjoyable to teach and have in their university. So sell yourself first and foremost as a sparky, intelligent, interestingly teachable enthusiast for the subject(s) you are applying for. Everything else is secondary, however brilliant your sporting record, your Young Enterprise achievements, or your tap-dancing.

Try to be individual without going over the top. If you suspect lots of other people are going to be saying what you are thinking of saying (for example, 'I've always been interested in the ancient world, ever since I first opened a book of Greek myths'), then either don't say it or find some individual slant (for example, a particular myth, and problem it sets you, or the insight it gives you into the world of the Greeks). Try to avoid clichés and verdicts that sound as if you are only delivering them because you think it's expected, or because that's what you were told to say in an A level essay ('In my reading I have much enjoyed exploring the contrast between Catullus' coarse invective and the rhetorical wit of Ovid'). You should aim to demonstrate your skills and interests rather than just stating them, through specific examples.

Show that you have got a sense of the questions that are there to be asked, and the new territory you will be able to explore at university (but without becoming just mistily aspirational – this will just put them off). It is fine to talk about your extracurricular activities and successes, but try to make sure that what you say helps to show that you have the kinds of skill (like time management) that will also help you make a success of your studies and be an asset to the department.

If you have not been able to study the ancient world at school (for example, AS or A level work in ancient history or classical civilisation), it is important to show through other evidence that you are a suitable and interesting candidate. Demonstrate that you have an intelligent interest from activity outside formal study. This might include reading of Greek and Roman history and literature (preferably including ancient texts in translation, rather than only modern works of popular history), visits to archaeological sites and museums, and interest in ancient remains in Greece and Italy (and other relevant parts of the world, even if you have not managed to visit yet). Mention specifics – works of ancient literature, or of historical analysis, or places that you have found particularly intriguing – and say why. These may be followed up in interviews, so make sure that your interest is genuine!

You should also try to explain how the work you have done at school, even if not directly focused on the ancient world, has nevertheless equipped you, in terms of approach, to tackle the ancient world. You do not have to apologise for not (yet) knowing any Latin or Greek – most students in classical studies, ancient history and classical archaeology will be starting in exactly the same position.

Your Personal Statement is also the place to explain anything unusual in your qualifications so far. If you need to, give good reasons to show that your formal results so far give a misleading picture of your real abilities. Tutors know that accidents happen in exams, and are very ready to listen to well-documented explanations.

## Examples from specific Personal Statements (from King's College, London)

From candidates who have studied ancient languages at school:

> I have loved Latin since I began it at the age of nine.

✓ It is encouraging that you still enjoy ancient languages after lengthy study, and your background in the subject will stand you in good stead for university. You could add that you have been looking in new directions for your university career. What authors have you read and would you like to go on to read? How do you think they may fit in the wider history of the ancient world? Are there any themes (death and mourning, involvement in politics, descriptions of remote places) in the texts that you have read which you would like to explore further?

From candidates who have little school background in the study of the ancient world:

> My interest was first sparked by the myths of Greece and Rome . . . I am very interested in ancient warfare and the conquests of Alexander the Great.

✓ Your attention has, understandably, been attracted by certain prominent stories and figures and this is appreciated by the admissions tutor. But if you're considering studying this at university, try to contextualise the images you have of the ancient world more. What have you read in ancient texts about warfare? What further questions might you go on to ask about Alexander the Great? Is there a course at your preferred university which covers this period and which will offer you more?

From a candidate interested in classical archaeology:

> In my gap year, I will be studying for a foundation course in art at X Art School. I am interested in all periods of art history and I would particularly like to study the relationship between ancient sculpture and Renaissance art.

✓ Coming to the study of archaeology with a background in art, rather than science, can produce interesting and equally valid approaches. Your dedication to a whole year of fine art study will suggest to the admissions tutor that you might work well with visual analysis and respond in interesting ways to the ancient evidence. There can be very different kinds of archaeological study, however, and an interviewer might be interested in to what extent you're aware of this. An interest in art history would also be balanced by the practical experience of a British dig, for which you could volunteer.

**TOP TIPS**

**1** Be intelligently enthusiastic

**2** Make sure you know the details of the programmes you are applying for and that this is reflected in the body of the text

**3** Keep your Personal Statement focused on what will make you a rewarding student of your chosen subject

**4** Read through what you have written and correct it where necessary

**5** Back up what you say about yourself with evidence, from extended reading, fieldwork or other sources. Be prepared to defend yourself if called to interview

**6** If your choice of subject is a recent one and you have not had years to construct a relevant extracurricular CV, you can provide an equally encouraging and impressive substitute in your statement by talking in detail about relevant background reading and by describing the further preparatory study you may undertake – perhaps a summer school, independent language study (with course book), visits to local Roman sites or more exotic climes or volunteer work in a museum or site. The more detailed and worked-out these plans are, the better

 **THINGS TO AVOID**

**1** Being too vague in your explanations of interest: try to get to the point quickly and back it up

**2** Parroting second-hand opinions

**3** Going on at great length about activities and achievements that are irrelevant to your chosen course

##  RECOMMENDED READING AND WEBSITES

- Archaeological excavations of interest to classics: www.indiana. edu/~classics/AIA/internet/internet.html
- Classics at Oxford: www.classics.ox.ac.uk
- Classics at Durham: www.dur.ac.uk/classics
- Warwick University: www2.warwick.ac.uk/services/library/main/tealea/arts/classics/usefulwebsites

I am grateful for the support I received from King's College London (www.kcl.ac.uk/schools/humanities/classics) in preparing this profile. Other highly rated courses include those at the universities of Oxford, Cambridge, Durham, Edinburgh and Exeter.

# COMPUTER SCIENCE

**This profile was written using information from an admissions tutor at Royal Holloway, University of London. The information is useful to all applicants, but some of the advice is pertinent to that department in particular.**

##  SUBJECT OVERVIEW

Computers, the internet, the web and other digital technologies continue to transform the economy, the world of finance and many other aspects of society. This digital revolution is accelerating and will play a key role in shaping the future. Computer science lies at the heart of this transformation: it studies how any sort of information, whether it is music or biological sequence data, can be represented and processed digitally. Demand for good computer science graduates has never been higher: a degree in computer science equips you for many challenging, and sometimes very well paid jobs in fields like finance, computational biology and many areas of business. Research by the eSkills sector skills council for IT and telecoms shows that the employment market for IT careers is growing five times faster than the general economy; every year 140,000 new entrants to the IT and telecoms workforce are needed.

Computer science is an excellent preparation for many careers, both technical and non-technical, throughout commerce and industry because students acquire intellectual discipline and practical project completion skills, which are highly valued, as well as specific technical skills that are in great demand. These include:

- the ability to analyse complex problems
- the ability to acquire the skills needed to solve problems and to design and implement solutions
- programming skills, including networking and databases
- data analysis skills
- communication skills
- the ability to work in a team
- leadership skills and management ability
- literacy and numeracy
- presentation skills.

## WHAT SKILLS OR ATTRIBUTES DO ADMISSIONS TUTORS LOOK FOR IN A GOOD APPLICANT?

Computer science is a hard but rewarding discipline. Admissions tutors generally tend to look for students who have some sort of technical or mathematical background. Students without an A level (or equivalent) in a technical subject like maths, physics or economics often struggle with the more abstract thinking required in computer science. Most first years have no previous experience with programming but if students have some programming experience in a language such as C++ or Visual Basic, that is not just a markup or scripting language, that is a good selling point. Tutors also tend to look for some interest or enthusiasm for computers, even if this is quite general.

In terms of academic qualifications, departments vary and you need to do your research. However, as a general rule the better departments will expect grades of between AAB and BBB and most good candidates will have studied AS or A level Maths. Computer Science or ICT AS level and the other mainstream sciences are also preferred. However, do your research carefully to ascertain what each department requires.

Tutors want students who have the maturity and self-discipline to cope with the more autonomous nature of university life; students need to be able to manage their time, and balance the demands of the different courses. Students also need to be problem solvers; they need to be curious and independent minded. Students can show they have these personal qualities through the range of their extracurricular activities or part-time work.

# WHAT DOES A GOOD PERSONAL STATEMENT LOOK LIKE?

This statement is a composite of various Personal Statements:

> I have always been very interested in computers. When I was a child, I would often take things apart to see how they work. When I was 10 years old, I was given a computer for my birthday, and while I started off just playing games and so on with it, I soon became more interested in trying to understand how it worked. At first I would just write little macros in Visual Basic to do useful things, but then I taught myself Java, and have written some simple games using this as part of my school computer club. I am also very interested in graphics and Photoshopping pictures to make them more interesting. I have made several websites using PHP and CSS, and I spend a lot of time reading about computers on the web and in magazines. My current computer I built myself from parts, which was a very educational experience, especially as it didn't work to start off and I had to figure out why.
>
> I have a part time job at PC World where I work as part of a team providing technical support for customers. My hobbies include playing the piano for a number of years, and I have achieved grade 5. I play sometimes in a band with some friends. My other main interest is sport, especially cricket. I have been part of the school team for several years.
>
> Academically, I have always been interested in maths, and with my love of computers, computer science seems a natural choice. I chose Maths and Physics as two of my A levels, but not Computing as I didn't enjoy ICT much at GCSE level, because the course focused just on using programs rather than making them.
>
> I am hard working and well organised, and think I will be able to cope well with the demands of a hard degree like CS: I am looking forward to the challenges of university life, and I want to get a job working in IT when I graduate.

✓ This is a good Personal Statement, as the student gives some reasons why he wants to study CS, and illustrates his enthusiasm for the subject with concrete examples. He shows he has self-discipline, takes part in a range of activities and has a serious interest in computing.

## TOP TIPS

**1** Make sure that you emphasise your ability in the technical or mathematical subjects

**2** If you enjoy puzzles, chess, card games such as poker or bridge and mental arithmetic puzzles such as Sudoku, say so

**3** If you have knowledge of programming, even at a fairly basic level, point this out: write about programs you have written and why

**4** If you are studying computer science at school, say what you particularly enjoyed that led you to apply for a degree level qualification. Read one of the suggested books and mention what you learnt from the book

**5** Sell yourself in a compelling and interesting manner: write clearly and concisely

## THINGS TO AVOID

**1** Spelling and punctuation mistakes

**2** Lying or plagiarism

**3** Underselling your achievements

**4** Saying you are only interested in gaming: you may be but this should be counterbalanced with your other interests

## RECOMMENDED READING AND WEBSITES

- David Harel and Yishai Feldman, *Algorithmics: The Spirit of Computing*, Addison-Wesley, 2004
- Hilary Nickell, *Careers Uncovered: The Internet*, Trotman Publishing, 2009
- Douglas R Hofstadter, *Godel, Escher, Bach: An Eternal Golden Braid*, Penguin, 2000
- Eric S Raymond, *The Cathedral and the Bazaar: Musings on Linux and Open Source*, O'Reilly Media, 2001

■ Cliff Stoll, *The Cuckoo's Egg: Tracking a Spy Through the Maze of Computer Espionage*, Pocket Books, 2005

I am grateful for the support I received from Royal Holloway (www.cs.rhul.ac.uk) in the composition of this profile. Other highly rated courses include those at universities such as Southampton, Cambridge, York, Surrey and Essex.

# DRAMA AND THEATRE STUDIES

**This academic profile was written using information provided by an admissions tutor at Royal Holloway, University of London. The information is useful to all applicants, but some of the advice is pertinent to that department in particular.**

## SUBJECT OVERVIEW

Drama is a much sought-after and stimulating degree programme. It is the study of performance, and performance pervades all aspects of public and private existence. Performance is also about communication and we live in a society where communications are vitally important. Studying drama at university explores human interaction both in the present and in the past. It is an ancient art form of social practice, through which we can develop an understanding of society today. Drama as a form of cultural practice offers ways in which to express ideas about human life.

Students explore these through a variety of modes of study, active as well as sedentary, group-based as well as individual, spoken as well as written, analytical as well as creative.

The study of drama and theatre provides you with useful life and employment skills, because of its emphasis on teamwork, planning projects, rigorous research and imaginative presentation.

A degree programme aims to teach as full a range of skills as possible, from the academic expertise of research and theoretical reading and writing to practical theatre skills. Students develop an inquisitive and questioning attitude to all aspects of the discipline. Specifically, students will gain skills in a variety of communications: writing logbooks and more traditional essays, presenting seminars, listening to peers' presentations and being able to pinpoint arguments that need further teasing out, and presenting performance work. Written skills in essay writing, logbook entries, review writing and bibliographic skills are also taught and assessed. Analytical skills in close textual reading, theoretical application and performance analysis are also gained. The skills of a drama graduate are easily transferable to other environments and are therefore highly sought after by employers.

 ## WHAT SKILLS OR ATTRIBUTES DO ADMISSIONS TUTORS LOOK FOR IN A GOOD APPLICANT?

Admissions tutors look for someone who has the ability to question. They are not looking for 'knowledge' of the subject because that merely tells them about the teaching that a candidate has received up to this point and not about the candidate themselves. So they are looking for potential.

Candidates need to demonstrate an interest in theatre, but this does not have to be in performing. Many university courses in drama are not concerned with developing acting abilities but rather fostering skills in group work, analysis, cultural engagement, and the bringing together of theoretical and practical exploration.

Admissions tutors like candidates who are good group members: this might be shown socially by the range of activities the student undertakes. They are also looking to match students to courses: for example, someone who wants to train to be an actor would be better applying for those courses; many university courses are about studying drama in a wider context and would be frustrating for those who want specialist training (and have perhaps applied to academic university courses because their parents want them to).

# WHAT DOES A GOOD PERSONAL STATEMENT LOOK LIKE?

## Example of a good Personal Statement

I wish to study theatre/performance at university due to the passion I have for drama. What evokes this passion is the unique way drama allows exploration of the human condition, its history, its philosophies and beliefs and emotions therein. My enthusiasm has developed through practical investigation of Miller, Fo, Shakespeare, Brecht and more recently, Artaud and Grotowski. My understanding of theatre has been greatly enhanced by my English Literature A level studies, through which I have broadened my knowledge of theatre history and revolutionary playwrights such as Marlowe. My understanding of photography has helped me to be creative and expressive in my work and to use imagery effectively. This has aided my study of drama, particularly in devised work. At university I desire to continue to learn, explore and further develop my performance skills and my understanding of the world of theatre.

I have aspirations to teach drama or to work in theatre. In the light of this I have applied for a nine-month placement in Tanzania teaching English and drama in African schools. I feel participating in such a scheme will help me to mature further and develop communication skills and subject knowledge. I am a very self-motivated person who enjoys getting involved in extracurricular activities. For example, in November I played Ophelia in the school production of Hamlet. During this process I gained a greater appreciation of how the theatre works and how much effort goes into putting on a show. This understanding was further developed in April when I was given the role of deputy stage manager in a school production of The Threepenny Opera. I am also a member of the school chamber choir and jazz choir.

✓ This statement shows someone who can think about the importance of drama within a wider context; the candidate is able to think about some of the functions of drama and also how their other A levels have broadened their understanding. The gap year activities are pertinent to the subject and challenging. The candidate's interest in drama goes beyond acting or self-interest: the lead female role in *Hamlet* provided a chance to think more about production aspects. The candidate shows that social activities have developed a sense of group membership.

## TOP TIPS

**1** Indicate that you are aware that drama and theatre studies at university tend to combine the

## THINGS TO AVOID

**1** Poorly constructed sentences with no clear direction or purpose academic study of theatre with performance skills. Some courses place very little emphasis on performance. You need to express clearly that you understand the distinction between performance arts and theatre studies and make it clear that you believe that this is right for you

**2** Illustrate your experience of performance with reference to live acts you have seen and how they have extended your knowledge of the subject

**3** Talk about the skills you have learnt from your study of drama or theatre studies thus far

**4** Emphasise the fact that you are personally motivated and willing to work hard independently to achieve your goals

**5** Detail the non-academic interests you have, especially if they involve working in an environment that promotes personal leadership and the need to overcome challenges without direct adult control, for instance the Duke of Edinburgh's Award

**2** Spelling, grammar and punctuation errors

**3** A statement that indicates that you have little understanding of the demands of the course and an awareness of the distinction between acting and drama/ theatre studies

**4** Making any claims that you would struggle to defend if called to interview or audition: that means no barefaced lies or blatant plagiarism of statements you might find on the internet. Be yourself!

# RECOMMENDED READING AND WEBSITES

- David Wiles, *A Short History of Western Performance Space*, Cambridge University Press, 2003
- Emma Govan, Helen Nicholson and Katie Normington, *Making a Performance: Devising Histories and Contemporary Practices*, Routledge, 2007

- Alison Hodge, *Twentieth Century Actor Training*, Routledge, 2000
- The writings by practitioners such as Peter Brook or Augusto Boal are accessible and help shed light on different aspects of theatre

I am grateful for the support of Royal Holloway (www.rhul.ac.uk/drama) in the preparation of this profile. Other highly rated courses include those at UEA, the Guildhall School of Music and Drama, Queen Mary and Central School.

# ENGINEERING (CIVIL)

**This academic profile was written using information provided by an admissions tutor at Southampton University and focuses on civil engineering as a single honours discipline. Engineering as a discipline at university is varied in its focus. Courses on offer include mechanical, aeronautical, structural, electrical and civil engineering. Each deals with a different aspect of human engineering needs and will require different skills, academic qualifications and interests. The information here is useful to all applicants, but some of the advice is pertinent to Southampton in particular.**

## SUBJECT OVERVIEW

Civil engineering applies science, mathematics, design and creativity to solve problems of critical importance to society, across construction, maintenance and management of infrastructure. We tend to take for granted the buildings we live and work in, the roads, railways and airports that allow us to travel, and the water that we use. It is professional civil engineers who make all this possible, and who are called on to find solutions to the major challenges facing the world in the future, such as the effects of climate change and sea level rise, finding sustainable sources of energy and dealing with congestion.

These degree courses provide excellent preparation, in terms of knowledge and understanding and key transferable skills, for a career in civil engineering. Many courses are fully accredited by the Institution of Civil

Engineers and the Institution of Structural Engineers, providing the first stage in a recognised career path to chartered or incorporated engineer status. Employment prospects are excellent.

# WHAT SKILLS OR ATTRIBUTES DO ADMISSIONS TUTORS LOOK FOR IN A GOOD APPLICANT?

The essential academic skills we look for are numeracy, problem-solving ability and logical thinking. Most entry requirements therefore include A level Mathematics and a science, or equivalent qualifications. Some top schools are likely to expect an A* in Maths or Physics A level from 2010 onwards. We also look for good communication skills in our students, both written and verbal. Other positive attributes are IT skills, a practical hands-on attitude to situations, and design flair and creativity, particularly for the civil engineering with architecture course.

Where at all possible, any evidence of work experience in an engineering environment should be promoted. It need not be long or high powered, but it will show a genuine interest in this vocation. One good taster course is the well-respected Headstart course.

Important personal qualities for a professional engineer are teamworking skills and leadership ability, evidence of potential which we can look for in candidates' Personal Statements, where they describe sporting activities, clubs, societies, hobbies, voluntary activities or business games in which they have been actively involved.

# WHAT DOES A GOOD PERSONAL STATEMENT LOOK LIKE ?

**Explain why you wish to pursue the particular line of study.**

You should give here a brief background on why you wish to pursue a career in civil engineering. This could be related to a family link, for example working in the family's construction business, or other experiences, for instance seeing structures while on holiday, articles in books/journals/engineering press, work experience.

**Describe the efforts you have already made to further your knowledge and understanding in the area.** Good applications always describe what steps the candidate has taken to find out more about the subject area. This is best done through practical experiences in the form of work experience placements with engineering firms, attending guest lectures, or participating in an engineering Headstart course at a university. You should briefly describe what you got out of the experience and how it has influenced you to apply for the course.

**Describe other attributes that demonstrate your wider 'generic' skills set.** Describe any relevant work experience you have had and how it has improved your communication, negotiation and team-building skills; for example, care in the community, shop work, engineering placements. Sporting achievements, clubs and society memberships, vocational qualifications and particularly any positions of responsibility taken within those areas should be highlighted; for example being a member of a football team, Duke of Edinburgh's Awards. Any charity work can also be mentioned.

**Link your generic skills set to the needs of your chosen course.** A good Personal Statement will go that step further and state how the skills learned through your generic skills will benefit you during your course; for instance, leadership or teamworking skills gained through a part-time job or while on a charity bike ride could help in undergraduate group projects or on a work placement.

 **TOP TIPS**

**1** Present all your qualifications clearly and accurately

**2** Write a succinct and clear Personal Statement, with a clear direction and flow from one point to another. Keep it concise and precise, promoting your skills in a compelling and interesting way

 **THINGS TO AVOID**

**1** Ambiguous or missing information

**2** Spelling or grammatical errors

**3** Thinking that engineering is about fixing things such as washing machines or cars

**3** Demonstrate your understanding of what engineering is about, preferably drawing on examples of engineering that you have read about or personally experienced. What motivated your interest in this subject?

**4** Demonstrate that you are interested in applying maths and science to real problems: mention the fact that you enjoy puzzles, mental arithmetic and designing

**5** Demonstrate in your statement activities that you have taken part in that show team working and leadership skills

**4** Saying that you can't wait to move away from anything involving maths and science

**5** Saying that your favourite hobby is going out with friends or watching the television: this is too often repeated and appears lazy and ill-prepared

# RECOMMENDED READING AND WEBSITES

- Construction News: www.cnplus.co.uk
- www.headstartcourses.org.uk – the website of the excellent taster courses in Engineering and Science. Well worth looking at if you have the time and inclination.
- Institution of Civil Engineers: www.ice.org.uk
- New Civil Engineer: www.nce.co.uk

I am grateful to Southampton University (www.southampton.ac.uk/ses) for their support in the preparation of this profile. Other highly rated courses can be found at the universities of Sheffield, Imperial College, Edinburgh, Nottingham and Dundee.

# ENGLISH

This academic profile was written using information provided by admissions tutors at Royal Holloway, King's College, Queen Mary's, all three part of the University of London. The information is useful to all applicants, but some of the advice is pertinent to Royal Holloway, King's and Queen Mary's in particular.

## SUBJECT OVERVIEW

English is a versatile and interesting subject, characterised by the rigorous critical study of literature and language. It is concerned with the production, reception and interpretation of written texts, and with the literary and expressive potential of the English language. The study of English demands a constant commitment to improving your reading and writing skills. It develops a flexible and responsive openness of mind and advanced skills in argument, and encourages you to think critically for yourself about literature and life.

In the first year most students take a common set of courses that introduce them to some of the major areas of literary study and provide them with an historical understanding of literature that stretches back as far as medieval times. This gives students the basis to progress to more advanced, specialised study of particular areas. In the second and third years, students are able to choose from a number of optional courses as wide-ranging as science fiction to Afro-American literature.

It is vital to research each department carefully and find out what they expect from you. If you love American literature, then do not apply to a department with no particular interest in that genre. This lazy approach will often lead to rejection in what is a very competitive application process. Take your time to choose the courses carefully and do not be swayed by the 'name' of the university.

A degree in English trains the mind and feeds the imagination; it provides a range of transferable skills, including oral and written presentation skills.

# WHAT SKILLS OR ATTRIBUTES DO ADMISSIONS TUTORS LOOK FOR IN A GOOD APPLICANT?

Admissions tutors will always consider the level of attainment in GCSEs and predicted grades for A levels first of all. Many English courses now demand very high grades, simply due to supply and demand. It is not at all uncommon for candidates to be made offers of AAB or higher. Equally, it is not unusual for candidates to be rejected from one or more of their preferred universities. However, it is also possible to get into English courses with lower grades. Do your research carefully!

Many course admissions tutors take into account the GCSE profiles of candidates. They look for evidence of consistent academic performance across a range of subjects. They tend to look favourably on candidates with one or more GCSE passes in a modern or ancient language. If you do not have a modern or ancient language pass, you, or preferably your referee, should explain the reason in your UCAS application.

In addition to the English A level, a good department will look for academic ability across a range of other subjects. They may look favourably on candidates with a profile balanced more towards the arts and humanities. Nonetheless, it is important that candidates choose subjects in which they have a genuine interest, rather than taking them for strategic purposes. Successful applicants in recent years have studied subjects such as history, French, German, philosophy, film studies, politics and maths.

The Personal Statement and school reference are then read for any signs that interest in English is not just a narrow product of quite enjoying it at A level. Tutors would hope to see indications of long-standing enjoyment, and an understanding that English at university will not be like three more years of A level English, but will be more demanding and unpredictable. We want to see evidence of wide reading and an appreciation of different literary genres.

Good applicants demonstrate excellent academic potential, demonstrated by their strong A level or equivalent grades, and enthusiasm for further study.

They show good time management and teamwork skills; the one to manage independent study successfully, the other to work co-operatively in seminars and group projects.

## WHAT DOES A GOOD PERSONAL STATEMENT LOOK LIKE?

A good Personal Statement introduces your real passions and personality. Just as every student is different, so every statement should also be different. However, more successful statements will demonstrate a sincere love of literature that goes beyond the set texts at school. Cultural interests, widely defined, should appear, such as theatre-going, gallery-visiting, films and music (if applicable).

> **During August, I volunteered to work as a literacy support assistant at my local library.**

✓ This is an example of real commitment to literature. The applicant saw reading as something of such utility and social value that she was helping others to begin.

Good statements also make it clear that the candidate wants to study literature and is interested in the kind of programme offered at a particular university.

QMUL also stresses the importance of the Personal Statement, which will help determine whether an applicant will be offered an interview. According to Dr Reid, a senior admissions tutor, your statement should illustrate dedication and enthusiasm to the subject area. He looks in particular for:

**❝** an indication of intellectual and cultural interests, along with evidence of commitment to the subject area, and liveliness and independence of mind. **❞**

He also makes the point that for a department which interviews applicants, an effective Personal Statement is especially important because, more often than not:

**❝** We use this part of the UCAS application as a starting point for discussion during the academic interview. **❞**

Dr Cornelia Cook, head of admissions for English, says that they are looking for 'evidence of wide and engaged reading', and ultimately, a real commitment to the subject. And finally, if you do not want to be humiliated at interview (and not many applicants do), you need to be prepared to discuss anything mentioned in your Personal Statement, including any texts. This could prove tricky if you have exaggerated your achievements and/or fabricated hobbies to make yourself sound more interesting.

 **TOP TIPS**

**1** The Personal Statement is an important discriminatory tool and therefore it should be prepared with care and attention to detail

**2** Emphasise early on a genuine passion for literature, reinforcing this with evidence that you have read widely and beyond the remit of the A level syllabus. If you mention an author you must be prepared to discuss this author's work if called to interview!

**3** Admissions tutors look for clear evidence of liveliness and independence of mind

**4** Clearly express the skills that you have learnt from the study of English and other subjects to A level or their equivalent

**5** Tell the tutor about the extracurricular pursuits you enjoy, but avoid just listing them. Concentrate on one or two activities that you feel particularly passionate about, and then tell them why and what you have

 **THINGS TO AVOID**

**1** Poor spelling, punctuation, grammar and sentence construction: this is English, after all!

**2** Failing to express your passion for English and not reinforcing it with examples that go beyond the remit of your A level course

**3** Exaggerating your achievements and/or making up hobbies to make you sound more interesting: if you do not want to be humiliated at interview, you need to be prepared to discuss anything mentioned in your Personal Statement, including any texts learnt from the pursuit of these activities

---

**6** Read as widely as possible, in particular other works by the authors you are studying, beyond the set texts. Experiencing performances of classic theatre, such as Shakespeare, or opera, would be beneficial

---

## RECOMMENDED READING AND WEBSITES

■ Explore some of the major works of pre-20th century literature – novelists such as Henry Fielding, Jane Austen, George Eliot, Charles Dickens; poets such as Donne, Wordsworth, Coleridge and Keats

I am grateful to the English departments at Queen Mary's (www.english.qmul. ac.uk), King's College (www.kcl.ac.uk/schools/humanities/depts/english) and Royal Holloway (www.rhul.ac.uk/english) for their support in compiling this profile. Other highly rated courses include those at the universities of Oxford, Cambridge, Durham, Glasgow and Leeds.

# ENVIRONMENTAL SCIENCE

This profile was written using information provided by an admissions tutor at Southampton University. Environmental science as a discipline is offered in a variety of different guises. These include single honours courses, environmental earth sciences, geophysical sciences and environmental geography. Each relates to a different aspect of this branch of science and will require different skills, academic qualifications and interests. The information here is useful to all applicants, but some of the advice is pertinent to Southampton in particular.

# SUBJECT OVERVIEW

Environmental sciences directly addresses the major and pressing issues facing human beings and the world we live in. Such problems have become regular headline news items over the last few years and include climate change, tsunamis, deforestation, pollution, destruction of wildlife, earthquakes and genetically modified organisms (GMOs).

At the same time it allows students to study for an interdisciplinary degree, cutting across the boundaries between traditional science subjects like biology, chemistry, geography, geology and oceanography, usually with a large practical and field-based element.

This is a growing area of career employment opportunity and the skills of an environmental scientist can now be used in many fields in the private and public sector.

Most degrees are modular, with a series of modules taken each year, building annually to increase the specialisation and complexity. Students often take a residential field course in Year 1 to develop practical skills and can take a further residential field course in Year 3, which is more student-led involving extensive field data collection and reporting.

# WHAT SKILLS OR ATTRIBUTES DO ADMISSIONS TUTORS LOOK FOR IN A GOOD APPLICANT?

Academic skills include communication (oral and written), team skills, numeracy and some evidence of scientific practical skill is normally preferred. Non-academic skills include independence, commitment and resilience.

The A level requirements vary from department to department. However, as a general rule most good departments will expect grades of between AAB and BBC. They will almost certainly expect at least one science A2 level (or equivalent), with preference given to biology and chemistry. Other good subjects include maths, geography, geology and physics.

# WHAT DOES A GOOD PERSONAL STATEMENT LOOK LIKE?

**Demonstrate your knowledge and enthusiasm:** say why you really want to do this degree, what has inspired you and why. If you have been involved in any relevant activities, through school or college, or perhaps through voluntary work, you should tell us about that, too. Do tell admissions tutors about other things as well. If you are interested in sport or music, that's fine, and achievement in non-academic areas can impress and show you are a good all-rounder. But focus mainly on your interest in the degree, and why this is what you want to do, including any aspirations for future careers.

## Example of a good Personal Statement

> The environment is something I have always been passionate about. From an early age I have watched wildlife in our garden, observing the annual cycles of life. At the same time I have always been committed to taking positive steps to help our environment – getting my parents to recycle their newspapers and switching to low-energy light bulbs when I was still at primary school. Since then my knowledge has expanded and my commitment has grown. I was chairman of a student group that helped my school gain Eco School status in 2006, and I was co-ordinator of our conservation group, creating a nature trail in the school grounds and working as volunteers on local nature reserves. I am also a member of my local Friends of the Earth group, and have been actively involved in their recent campaigns about overfishing, including attending a large demonstration in London.

✓ This demonstrates long-term commitment to issues relevant to the degree.

> My inspiration has increasingly come from my studies and the reading I have done to support them. I have immersed myself in the works of Aldo Leopold such as Sand County Almanac – although these were written in the first half of the last century, the lessons about prudent use of our world's resources apply more than ever today.

✓ Good evidence of academic commitment and knowledge, well written.

> Inspired by work such as that, and by the global leadership of Al Gore and the Intergovernmental Panel on Climate Change, I now want to study for a degree that will both challenge me intellectually and lead to a worthwhile and rewarding career.
>
> I chose my A levels in Chemistry, Geography and Biology with an environmental sciences degree in mind. I enjoy practical work, both in the laboratory and in the field, and put them to good use in a work placement last summer in the Environment Agency's laboratories, analysing water quality.

✓ Relevant to this type of course, and an indication of skills.

> Our field trip to Belize changed my life – the wealth of environmental riches in Latin America is truly astounding – with coral reefs, rainforests and wildlife, as well as remarkable local cultures – but the threats they may face in future years from the activities of humans is alarming.

✓ Good example, nicely summarised.

> I hope one day to work in research into managing conservation areas in developing countries, and have taken Spanish AS level this year to help develop some useful language skills.

✓ Shows forward planning, strategic thinking and some ambitious career aspirations.

> I am a member of my local football team, and have been captain for the last two years, which has given me additional responsibility in getting everyone to work together – we were the first girls' team set up in our town and have been together for five years, and won the County Cup in 2007. I take an interest the arts as well – I play jazz piano in a band at college and we have performed in local music festivals. I hope to continue some sports and music at university.

✓ Evidence of ability as a team player, also of self-management.

## Example of a poor Personal Statement

> I think an environmental sciences degree would be really good for me to study. It will be really interesting to find out more about our world.

✗ No depth here.

> I became interested in this when I realised that I wasn't going to get good enough grades to study to be a vet at university.

✗ Not a good admission to make.

> I have since noticed how much things like climate change are on the TV news.

✗ Not specific enough.

> I have always been interested in animals, and keep reptiles at home, and would like to learn more about them and how they behave.

✗ So does he still want to be a vet really?

> I am taking Biology and Geography A levels along with music because it is the other thing I am very interested in. I play guitar for an indie rock band called Armageddon Death Bomb, which I started with some friends at school. We have worked really hard, and practise most days, which can make it difficult to keep up with school work. We are hoping to play at some festivals this summer and if we do well I might take a gap year to see if we can be successful.

✗ This shows commitment, but not to anything academic or relevant to the degree, and suggests that university is actually plan B if the music career doesn't take off.

> To keep fit I skateboard, and I use my board to get around which saves money and is a sustainable form of transport. I also like to go surfing, so am interested in studying at a university near the sea.

✗ Inappropriate as a main choice of university, although it might be one factor to consider. This is also very short – use the space provided.

##  TOP TIPS

**1** In the opening paragraph, let the tutor know why it is that you have been drawn towards the subject and what evidence you can provide that indicates that you have an understanding of the demands of the course

**2** Let them know about any extended reading or fieldwork opportunities that you might have had or any extracurricular interests that pertain to the degree specifically, for example conservation projects or recycling initiatives

**3** Promote your existing skills in science-based subjects and other related subjects such as geography

**4** Show that you are aware of the current issues that relate to

##  THINGS TO AVOID

**1** Spelling and punctuation mistakes: get your statement proofread carefully

**2** Lies or claims that you would struggle to defend in an interview

**3** Copying someone else's statement: we want to get to know you, not them!

**4** Too much emphasis on interests that are irrelevant to your chosen course

**5** Not using up the full amount of space: this leaves a bad impression unless the rest of the statement is outstanding the subject and that you read quality journalism and literature. Mention any particular area of the subject that particularly interests you and explain why

**5** Give some indication that you are an independent learner with the personal initiative required to thrive in this environment

**6** Tell us about your interests beyond school and college

---

## RECOMMENDED READING AND WEBSITES

- Works by authors such as Richard Dawkins, Steve Jones, James Lovelock, Aldo Leopold, Rachel Carson are good for general reading around the subject
- *New Scientist*: www.newscientist.com
- Quality newspapers for environmental news stories or editorials

I am grateful to the Environmental Science department at Southampton (www.civil. soton.ac.uk/es) for their support in compiling this profile. Other highly rated courses include those at the universities of Leicester, Manchester, Imperial College and UEA.

# FINE ART AND ART FOUNDATION

This academic profile was written using information provided by an admissions tutor from Dundee University (which includes the Duncan Jordanstone College). The information in this profile is useful to all applicants, but please be aware that some of the advice is pertinent to that department in particular.

# SUBJECT OVERVIEW

Students wishing to study fine art at university normally undertake a one-year foundation programme first which equips them to apply for a three-year BA honours degree in fine art. In Scotland students enter a four-year degree programme in art or design, the first year of which is normally a diagnostic General Foundation in Art and Design.

The first aim of a foundation course is the development of your ability, skill and critical faculties by means of thoughtful study and visual outcomes. An awareness of the broad nature of art and design underlies the teaching of the course. The process of acquiring sound basic skills includes consideration of creativity, aesthetics, visual awareness, and analytical and critical faculties. Knowledge and a sense and understanding of the history, theory and practice of art and design is cultivated, allowing you to place yourself, your work and aspirations in context.

The second aim is to help you decide from the varied modules undertaken, your choice of degree study for the subsequent three years. The make-up of the modules has been carefully devised to enable you to gain a broad experience, awareness and skill level allied to art and design practices.

Parallel to this is the contribution the overall dynamics of the course, as a learning experience, make to the progressive development of your sense of connection to a specific area of subject specialism.

These twin aims are achieved through students working alongside each other in studios on projects led by academic staff.

During their foundation year students will apply to the degree specialism of their choice. This will involve preparing an application and accompanying portfolio. Students may be invited for an interview. The selection process will identify students who will benefit from a fine art education. The aims of a fine art programme include:

- to offer students the opportunity to develop their potential as independent artists in a multidisciplinary culture and an atmosphere of creative innovation and endeavour
- to produce graduates who are confident in their chosen areas of practice, who have developed visual imagination and awareness, and have acquired many personal and interpersonal, professional, transferable and research skills
- to develop the student's understanding of the artistic, historical, theoretical and cultural context which informs and shapes practice
- to develop the student's critical and self-critical capacities.

Students on fine art programmes may specialise in one particular discipline, such as sculpture, but increasingly students work across a range of visual disciplines in pursuit of the visualisation of their ideas. They will have opportunities to participate in study visits and to display their work in exhibitions. Most degree programmes will culminate in an annual public degree exhibition.

 **WHAT SKILLS OR ATTRIBUTES DO ADMISSIONS TUTORS LOOK FOR IN A GOOD APPLICANT?**

Your portfolio will be considered to assess your enthusiasm, creativity, intellectual and practical skills in the practice of art and design. Consideration will be given to your potential for further development and progress in any of the fields of art and design the college has to offer.

The selector(s) will also be looking for indications of your visual awareness, the range of your interests and experience and the level of your commitment to art and design. Your portfolio should include representative examples of work undertaken as part of a programme of study. The compilation of a portfolio should not be regarded as an end in itself, but rather as one of the results of that study. It is the primary means by which you present yourself to the selector, so you should prepare it accordingly.

# WHAT DOES A GOOD PERSONAL STATEMENT LOOK LIKE?

Your portfolio is the primary tool for the selection process, but your Personal Statement adds a valuable context. It should be imaginative and creative. You should demonstrate creativity and a desire to pursue a career in art. Admissions tutors are interested in hearing about school and extracurricular activities, but only where they demonstrate in a broader context how they have helped develop you as a person in relation to your artistic aspirations.

## Examples from good Personal Statements

> Having been involved in and thoroughly enjoyed art and design during my years at school, culminating in advanced Higher Art and Design and portfolio this year, I am now sure that my chosen future career will be art-related.

✓ This is a clear, unambiguous and honest opening sentence.

> It may seem unoriginal but the arts have always been an important part of my life. I would describe myself as a creative person and am interested in the links between the visual arts and language. To quote artist Jackson Pollock, 'It is all a big game of construction – some with a brush, others choose a pen.'

✓ This opening shows a wider awareness of the cultural context of art. It also demonstrates an appreciation of the links between different aspects of creative arts.

> Summer of 2006 enabled me to address my future and determine my choice of study. It was during that time that I realised that my interests in both art and computer graphics could be combined. I was very lucky to get the opportunity to work with a games company as a games tester. I gained invaluable experience in learning how the business side of the industry worked as well as the creative process.
>
> During my fifth year at school I found the higher art course enjoyably challenging. I had to work to strict deadlines on two units – jewellery design, producing a piece inspired by the Botanic Gardens, and portraiture, which involved painting a self-portrait. I also learned about several painters from different movements. During that year I also attended a summer school at a local college and went on to join a life drawing class and portfolio building class.

✓ These two examples demonstrate the initiative and commitment shown through a wider involvement with art-related studies beyond the school or FE curriculum.

Outside of college I have a part-time job in Asda where I interact with many different types of people, colleagues and customers. This job has helped me improve my communication skills in day-to-day life and to become more confident. At school I enjoyed the challenge of being the chair of a school committee which organised events to raise money for charity both in and outside school. For example, we raised funds for Red Nose Day and I was involved in making posters to raise awareness as well as making a short film which was shown to various year groups to encourage fellow pupils and staff to give money.

✓ An individual demonstrating how they invest their creative abilities in a wider context.

I was also a prefect, a role from which I learned better timekeeping and became more mature and responsible. I also developed other skills during my time in sixth year through helping a first year academically and socially as part of the buddying system. Not only did I enjoy this but I learned to listen and be patient and to be aware of how other people use situation.

✓ An acknowledgement of the collective responsibility and contribution that can be made in a community. It also displays an awareness of the personal attributes acquired through taking on roles of responsibility

I decided I wanted to study art so I looked at various course options. I had heard that particular courses were excellent so I took the opportunity to go to their open days. I was particularly attracted by the course at . . . and the foundation year seemed a good way to discover which area of art would suit me. However, at present I feel I would like to pursue sculpture.

✓ Shows that the applicant has seriously researched the options available and made a considered choice of application.

The following statement stood out from the crowd – it was the second year that the student had applied and this statement played a strong supporting role to her portfolio in the decision to offer her a place. She is now studying graphic design.

Me? I love: unexpected snow, my friends, surprises, gifts, noodles, music, computing, socialising, writing, spontaneity, the smell of petrol/bleach/vanilla, strawberry jam, old photographs, my family, meddling, new socks, guitars, being random, driving through puddles, heavy rain, apple juice, gigs, camping, tartan mini skirts with hoodies and so much more, but above all else I love art. I know that may seem like one heck of a generalisation, but it's true. I love everything from paintings that seem like photographs (Michelangelo) to ones which verge on the obscure (Francis Bacon), sketches which must have taken hours (Da Vinci) to comic strips (John Allison), graffiti (Banksy) to elaborate sculptures (Mark Quinn) and everything in between!

This year I have been indulging and further extending my love for all things arty by attending Dundee College on a full-time portfolio course. Through this I feel that I have greatly enhanced my skills and knowledge in drawing, design and painting. In general I enjoy the expressive subjects more than design but on the whole I enjoy the whole course, with my favourite class changing every week! I also feel that my social and interpersonal skills have developed as I have made many new friends and had the chance to meet people who I otherwise would have not.

In particular my life drawing has come on tremendously. I currently attend a night course at college and am thoroughly enjoying it as I never had the chance to do it at school and I feel it helps, not just with my life drawing, but also other aspects of the subject. I also plan to start a night class on using Dreamweaver later in the year as I am particularly interested in the areas of graphic design and the internet.

Going to Dundee College has meant that I have had to give up my cleaning job as the hours were incompatible as I have to travel by train every day and I arrive home late at night but it's all been worthwhile.

Outside of college I enjoy going to various art galleries to look at what is happening in the art world and to see different exhibitions. I feel that it is important to have an interest in a wide variety of art as all aspects of it overlap and tie in with each other, so a technique used in fine art may in fact help with something in design. This way I feel that I am broadening the range of techniques and skills I have for the future.

Although the workload has been demanding this year I have found it a welcome change to school, where I was vice captain of my house and had to perform various duties such as organising house events and maintaining the house noticeboard (a harder task than it sounds when you get no help from your captain!). I was also in charge of the lockers, which meant I had to make sure they were properly maintained and distributed. All the duties I had to perform in secondary school have helped make me become more organised and more reliable. I also now know that I am capable of working not just in a team but I can also work on my own competently.

Overall I feel that I am ready to further my education by attending university, where I hope to continue to enjoy the subject as much as I have done in the past and to carry on learning and adding to my artistic abilities. I believe that I am a conscientious, organised and self-motivated person who will cope well with the demands of university life. Irrespective of my long-term career path, I am confident that my all-round abilities would serve me well in an art course. I am keen to broaden my horizons in an academic, social and personal sense and feel that university study will provide many opportunities for development.

## Examples from poor Personal Statements

It was clear to me from a very young age that art was my great passion, not only because I was told I was talented, but because I enjoyed everything about it. I was never happier than when spending all my hours in the school art department.

✗ This opening paragraph is a cliché – both in language and sentiment.

As a child I was deeply unhappy if I didn't have my crayons with me. In my spare time I like to read, sketch or paint. I get a real thrill and am inspired by producing a completely original piece of work. This feeling drives me to achieve my ambition at a much higher level.

✗ This comes across as being naïve. It reads as if this is a hobby rather than a serious commitment.

I was elected school prefect in my final year and was involved in an anti-bullying initiative. I also attend a local church and teach in the Sunday school.

For several years I attended karate lessons. At present I am in my second year of being a prefect at school, which is a very responsible position. I study a lot in my free time as well as working part time doing clerical work in a local office. In school I was asked by the learning support unit to assist students with learning difficulties with their school work.

✗ This is just a list of achievements with no acknowledgement of the skills they have developed through these activities.

 **TOP TIPS**

**1** Your portfolio is the primary tool for the selection process, but your Personal Statement adds a valuable context: it should be imaginative and creative

**2** Get someone else to read over your statement before you send it. It is very easy to overlook grammatical and spelling errors, lack of punctuation, repetition, and omitting vital information

**3** Emphasise your love of art and the artistic process: convey this passion in a way that is compelling and unusual

**4** Draw on what influences you know and any artist or artistic genre you find compelling

 **THINGS TO AVOID**

**1** Copying examples of Personal Statements you find on the web: you should only use them as a guideline. They are easy to spot and result in statements that do not show the individuality that selectors are looking for

**2** Using clichés and overtly 'arty' language

**3** Implying that art is a hobby, not an intellectual passion

**4** Telling lies and near-truths that can be exposed at interview

##  RECOMMENDED READING AND WEBSITES

■ Alan Pipes, *Foundations of Art and Design*, Laurence King Publishing, 2008

■ James Burnett, *Getting Into Art and Design Courses 2011 Entry*, 7th edition, Trotman Publishing, 2010

I am grateful for the support of Duncan Jordanstone College of Art & Design (www.djcad.dundee.ac.uk) in compiling this profile. Other highly rated courses can be found at the colleges such as Slade, Camberwell, Central School, Glasgow and Goldsmiths.

# GEOGRAPHY

This academic profile was written using information provided by an admissions tutor at Royal Holloway, University of London. The information in this profile is useful to all applicants, but some of the advice is pertinent to that department in particular.

##  SUBJECT OVERVIEW

Geography is a diverse and exciting subject, which allows students to explore and understand the key environmental, economic, social and political challenges we face in the modern world.

Learning about the environment, sustainable development, climate change, globalisation and other issues that affect our lives is an essential part of modern geography. The subject is unique in providing a bridge between the social sciences, with their understanding of the dynamics of societies, cultures and behaviour, and the environmental sciences with their understanding of physical landscapes and the dynamics of environmental processes. The interaction between people and the environment lies at the heart of the discipline and is essential to contemporary understanding of today's global problems.

By studying such a broad subject, students obtain a range of learning experiences and skills that make geography graduates highly attractive to future employers.

The Royal Geographical Society advocates that on completion of your degree you will have many skills in preparation for work. These will be integral to your training, and to your employability, and should include:

**Intellectual skills**, such as critically evaluating theories and judging evidence to make informed decisions and to develop reasoned arguments.

**Geography-specific skills** such as undertaking a piece of research using a range of technical methods for the collection and analysis of spatial and environmental data, and undertaking fieldwork.

**Key transferable skills** in communication, presentation, debate, numerical analysis, teamwork, problem-solving, report and essay writing and many IT skills.

**Personal attributes** such as time management, development of responsibility, coping with uncertainty, self-reflection, motivation, flexibility, and creativity.

# WHAT SKILLS OR ATTRIBUTES DO ADMISSIONS TUTORS LOOK FOR IN A GOOD APPLICANT?

We are looking for individuals who are passionate about geography and curious about the world in which we live. It is important that this interest goes beyond the confines of the curriculum and classroom, for example through attending outside lectures or reading geography-related books or magazines. They should be able to see how geography helps explain human and environmental processes in their everyday lives.

Studying at university requires students to be self-motivated and independent. Applicants need to have developed good communication skills that allow them to present information effectively in both written and oral forms. They also need to have good ICT and data analysis skills and be able to manage their time successfully and to work in groups.

Good applicants are well-rounded individuals who have interests beyond their school work. Activities such as sport, music and drama, as well as community work or paid employment, all involve skills development and will help you meet the challenges of university study.

# WHAT DOES A GOOD PERSONAL STATEMENT LOOK LIKE?

## Example from a good Personal Statement

From an applicant who wants to study a physical geography course.

I have always been fascinated with geography and the way in which landforms are created. I enjoy both physical and human geography, but my main interests lie in the physical aspects. Pursuing geography to degree level has been a logical step for me. I want to develop my knowledge of geomorphological and environmental processes and, after graduation, find employment in a related field in either an academic or commercial environment.

My school fieldtrip to Arran gave me the opportunity to investigate a very different landscape, and see the role of tectonic processes and glaciation in forming features such as sills and dykes, raised beaches and U-shaped valleys. I regularly attend Geographical Association lectures and particularly enjoyed a recent talk on coastal management in East Anglia. I also subscribe to Geography Review magazine, which helps develop my understanding of geography.

My other A level subjects complement my interest in geography. For example, biology has helped me when studying ecosystems and maths has been important in the statistical analysis of fieldwork data. In all my A level courses, I have developed my skills in presenting information in written and oral form and using ICT.

For my work experience, I spent a week in the environmental department of the local council, focusing on their work related to the sustainable management of rivers and floodplains. With the increasing demand for housing in my local area, it is vital that planners consider flood risk when making decisions about urban development. I attended community consultation meetings as well as analysing maps showing high-risk floodplain locations. Such work demonstrates the practical contributions that geography can make in improving our lives.

I am passionate about sport and have played football for my school team for the past five years. Last year I was selected to play at county level and I hope to continue playing at university. Combining sport and schoolwork requires good time management and organisation. Outside of school time I have a part-time job at my local supermarket. This has improved my self-confidence, teamwork and communication skills.

I believe that I am a hard-working and motivated student, who can prioritise and deal with workloads and deadlines. I can use my initiative and remain open-minded. I believe that university will allow me to become even more independent and will provide many opportunities to broaden my interests further. The chance to increase my knowledge in a subject that I enjoy immensely is extremely attractive.

The key aspects that make this a good Personal Statement are:

- a strong opening statement that shows why the applicant wants to study geography
- evidence that they understand what geography is about and what they have learned from their study of geography so far. Bringing in some details about the landforms of Arran helps support claims about being interested in landform formation
- including information about geography-related activities (going to Geographical Association lectures and reading *Geography Review*) demonstrates an interest and curiosity in the subject that goes beyond the classroom
- an awareness of how geography intersects with other subjects and what skills they have developed in their A levels
- recognition of how geography can be applied to real-world problems. This shows that they have thought about what geography is as a subject
- information about interests and work experience, and what skills they have helped the applicant to develop
- a final section summing up what personal qualities they have that make them suitable to study geography at university
- no spelling or grammar mistakes.

# TOP TIPS

**1** Indicate that you understand what geography is about and that you are aware of the demands of the course

**2** Show clearly any experience that you have of coursework and fieldwork and what they taught you

**3** Indicate an awareness of how geography intersects with other subjects and what skills you have gained from the study of your other A levels

**4** Provide evidence of your extracurricular pursuits, particularly where these indicate leadership potential or personal initiative

# THINGS TO AVOID

**1** Poor spelling, punctuation and grammar

**2** Underselling your current skills

**3** Indicating a poor understanding of the demands of the course due to poor research: for instance, confusing physical and human geography

---

# RECOMMENDED READING AND WEBSITES

- Peter Daniels, Michael Bradshaw, Denis Shaw and James Sidaway, *An Introduction to Human Geography: Issues for the 21st Century*, 3rd edition, Pearson, 2008

- Joseph Holden (ed), *An Introduction to Physical Geography and the Environment*, 2nd edition, Prentice Hall, 2008

- Paul Cloke, Philip Crang and Mark Goodwin (eds), *Introducing Human Geographies*, 2nd edition, Hodder Arnold, 2005

- *Geography Review* magazine. Published four times a year by Philip Allan (www.philipallan.co.uk)

■   The Royal Geographical Society with The Institute of British Geographers: www.rgs.org; http://studygeography.rgs.org

I am grateful for the support of Royal Holloway (www.gg.rhul.ac.uk) in the compiling of this profile. Other highly rated courses can be found at the universities of Cambridge, Oxford, Bristol, St Andrew's and Edinburgh.

# GEOLOGY

**This academic profile was written using information provided by an admissions tutor at Southampton University. The information in this profile is useful to all applicants, but some of the advice is pertinent to Southampton in particular.**

## SUBJECT OVERVIEW

An undergraduate degree in geology will involve many diverse, but integrated activities: lectures to provide theory and knowledge, laboratory practicals to teach fundamental analytical and practical skills, and fieldwork, both on one-day excursions and residential courses in the UK and abroad, to provide hands-on training in geological field techniques and mapping.

To understand the nature, dynamics and evolution of the physical, chemical and biological processes operating on the Earth over the past four billion years, a course will integrate aspects of most of the physical sciences: chemistry, physics, maths, biology and geography, producing all-round science graduates. All good courses will include instruction and practice in professional key skills such as report/essay writing, giving lectures and presentations and presenting papers and posters, all things you will be doing as a graduate scientist.

All of this information will be provided in a coherent and progressive manner, and there will be a huge variety of different assessment methods, from written and practical exams to teamwork projects, independent research, posters and oral presentations, all in a way that is accessible and enjoyable to all. Being taught by active researchers in their own field of expertise is always beneficial, because research scientists can be counted on not only to be enthusiastic about their subject and to pass on their enthusiasm to you, but also to provide instruction on cutting-edge topics that form the current focus of international investigation.

A diverse variety of course modules are the key to a good geology degree, and you should expect to be taught topics as diverse as biomolecular palaeontology and geological hazards, geochemistry and palaeoclimate change. You should expect to be challenged and have your abilities stretched throughout the duration of your degree, and be able to demonstrate that you can apply what you have learnt in problem-based exercises.

Fieldwork should be a key element; you should be taught how to use field equipment and how to collect, analyse and interpret a variety of different types of field data and samples. All degree courses accredited by the Geological Society of London will offer an independent mapping project of some form, taking the form of several weeks' worth of field surveying somewhere in the world, usually in the summer vacation between the second and third years of study. There will be support staff to guide and instruct you to successfully complete these specialised activities, but self-motivation and time management skills are also essential!

Most universities will provide opportunities for the most talented students to conduct a period of study abroad at a partner institution, and there will be many other opportunities for involvement in extracurricular or directly degree-related research activities to be incorporated into a geological degree. Above all, if you have a degree of independence, a great deal of drive and motivation for field-based activities, you will find a degree in geology to be a hugely rewarding experience.

# WHAT SKILLS OR ATTRIBUTES DO ADMISSIONS TUTORS LOOK FOR IN A GOOD APPLICANT?

Applicants should display a drive and enthusiasm for, and an informed understanding of the degree programme(s) for which they have applied, and should be able to demonstrate that they have thoroughly researched the subject area and have considered why they wish to undertake such a degree in the context of their future career development. Applicants will be expected to have ensured that their academic background and the examinations they are yet to secure are acceptable, and their qualifications will be of a sufficient level of attainment to ensure admission to the course of their choice.

The applicants should provide sufficient information in their Personal Statement to indicate that they not only appreciate the personal skills and abilities required for successful completion of an earth science degree, but that they can illustrate such an appreciation with pertinent personal examples in the form of educationally based experiences (for example, personal and team-based sporting or musical activities), extracurricular or work experiences. If an applicant can provide evidence or demonstrate well-developed time and personal management skills, English language, grammar and numerical skills, along with a degree of independence, these are all aspects of a candidate's character that will be of interest to admissions staff.

# WHAT DOES A GOOD PERSONAL STATEMENT LOOK LIKE?

Your Personal Statement should provide an admissions tutor with sufficient information to convey that you have not only a drive and enthusiasm for the degree programme(s) for which you are applying, but also that you have thoroughly researched the subject area and have considered why you wish to undertake such a degree in the context of your future career development. As a potential applicant you will be expected to tailor your Personal Statement to address your interest in the wider subject discipline and perhaps in specific areas of the discipline.

To realise this you may choose to draw upon your own experiences in AS/A2 level subjects, involvement in subject-related extracurricular activities or work experience. This part of the statement ought to comprise some 30–50% of the whole statement, and should be reflective and demonstrate self-awareness.

As all earth and marine science subject areas will have a practical, field-based component, you ought to highlight any such experience and skills which you already have, be it study-based (for example, A levels), or extracurricular (for example, Duke of Edinburgh's Award scheme, Operation Raleigh, or activity-style holidays you have organised for yourself). However, many of the personal skills and abilities required for successful completion of an earth or marine science degree can also be demonstrated by reference to other forms of education-based experience (for example, personal and individual/team-based sporting or musical activities), or work experience. Avoid meaningless literary quotes or apparent deep thoughtful insights about your chosen topic that you have picked off a website or invented – admission tutors have read most of them already!

## Example of a good Personal Statement

While one child may have picked up a rock and skimmed it across the sea, my inquiring mind would not let me do this – I had to know more about it: where it came from, how it was formed. As a young child I was fascinated by rocks and earth materials around me – as I grew older, learning about plate tectonics and earthquakes through secondary school intrigued me further. I am currently studying biology and chemistry, both of which have a strong affiliation to geology and have provided me with additional scientific skills applicable to my geography course. I came to understand more about igneous, sedimentary and metamorphic rocks, permeable and impermeable rocks and the properties of materials such as chalk and clay, and I have recently attended a geography masterclass at the University of X, where aspects of environmental geography were discussed and developed. I subscribe to Geology Today in which I have read articles such as 'From microscopic minerals to global climate change' by David J Brown and Martin Lee. Articles of this kind have provided me with more in-depth geologists' views on the causes of climate change.

I have recently conducted field trips to The Lizard in Cornwall, where one can stand up on the Moho, and up to the top of Mount Nephin in Ireland. It was in Ireland where I completed my pilot study, mapping a series of dykes inside a mainly metamorphic region. Earlier this year I went on fieldwork to Le Massif Central in France where I completed my coursework of mapping and deducing the geological history of the area around Lac Chambon, and it was in France that I finally realised the true scale to which I am amazed by volcanoes while stood at the top of Puie du Marie. On these trips I have gained valuable knowledge from the field and a first-hand understanding of geology. I especially enjoy the challenge of fieldwork, as I get the chance to explore new regions and broaden my ever expanding horizons, making the most of what I can achieve: be it climbing a rock face to investigate a mineral vein, or contemplating a geological map. I'm a very 'outdoors' person and adverse weather doesn't bother me!

My desire to obtain a glimpse into what life is like as a geological researcher drove me to apply for a position on a five-week expedition to Disko Island, off the western coast of Greenland this summer. While in Greenland we studied how glaciers had formed the valleys there, and mapped some of the geological data. The data we gathered about the movement of the snouts of the glaciers will be accessible to scientists around the world for research into climate change. This expedition allowed me to experience geological fieldwork further, improving my motivation and determination, and allowing me to develop as a person. The expedition also required me to raise over £4,500 in under a year, which I achieved through working part time, participating in a sponsored run and organising a first aid course for local mountaineers.

I have a fascination for the role played by geologists in the developing world, and the positive contribution of geologists to the crisis that we currently face as a global community is something that has inspired me very much. The scarcity of resources and the impact of global climate change are developments I find both worrying and fascinating, and I understand that there is particular demand for geologists who can make accurate decisions for governments and gas mining industry, or possibly civil or environmental engineering.

I have been actively involved in several projects in school, which I believe have provided me with the opportunities to mature as a young person. I am currently mentoring students in the year below me and helping them to achieve similar success. Last year I became a reading partner for younger students, which I feel greatly benefited them as well as giving me valuable experience in working sympathetically with younger children. In my spare time I enjoy participating in sports, and am a qualified RYA dinghy instructor and later this year will be completing my Basic Expedition leadership award, which will allow me to run Duke of Edinburgh's Award expeditions. I also enjoy supporting others, and was a prefect in the lower sixth and am currently on the senior prefect team at my school for upper sixth.

My voluntary teaching at my sailing club is recognised by the Millennium Volunteer Scheme, where I have so far spent over 150 hours volunteering. These hobbies have developed my leadership skills and have pushed me to manage my time effectively, so that I can make the most of all the opportunities open to me. Furthermore, I have had the opportunity to meet a wide range of people and learn important skills in leadership and communication. I feel I have the maturity and enthusiasm to appreciate the academic opportunities offered at university and I am looking forward to participating in the activities that are available.

✓ This Personal Statement covers all of the subjects that admissions tutors in this subject area wish to read about. There is evidence of the candidate's enthusiasm for the degree subject for which they have applied, and the statement illustrates their in-depth understanding and appreciation of the specific areas of the discipline. The applicant provides ample indications of their drive and interest in the subject by having made strenuous efforts to accumulate subject-based practical extracurricular experience (although we do not expect all applicants to offer such 'exotic' experience!). In later parts of the statement the applicant indicates very strong self-awareness of their own skills, abilities and limitations – and their willingness to push themselves in every aspect of their life – both academic and personal – invaluable information for someone trying to assess an applicant's aptitude for university-level studies.

 **TOP TIPS**

**1** Although this is not directly related to the statement, please ensure your qualifications meet published admissions criteria for the particular degree course for which you are applying (you'd be amazed at the number of applications that get rejected due to applicants applying without the correct subjects or numbers of qualifications)

**2** Provide honest and reflective comments about why you wish to study at university and what you want to achieve, as well as checking that your grammar and spelling are correct!

**3** Describe and evaluate as fully as possible what you gained from the coursework and fieldwork you have already completed as part of your school or college course

 **THINGS TO AVOID**

**1** Applying for courses without having checked you have the correct qualifications to offer

**2** Poor spelling and use of grammar

**3** If you are applying for several different but related subjects on your UCAS form, do not focus your Personal Statement on one of these to the detriment of the others: admissions tutors only see the degree course you have applied for at their individual institution and they will not be impressed if your statement focuses on a different course at another institution

**4** Trying to impress using literary quotes, or unlikely and apparently deeply thoughtful insights about your degree subject

# RECOMMENDED READING AND WEBSITES

- Geologists' Association: www.geologists.org.uk

I am grateful to the Geology department at the University of Southampton (www.soes.soton.ac.uk) for their support in compiling this profile.

# HISTORY

**This academic profile was written using information provided by an admissions tutor at Royal Holloway, University of London. The information in this profile is useful to all applicants, but some of the advice is pertinent to that department in particular.**

## SUBJECT OVERVIEW

With global societies changing at a rapid pace, history has perhaps never been so relevant. The study of history concerns our understanding of what it was to be human in another place and at another time. Exploring what others have felt, thought, and done in the past expands our self-awareness and our understanding of how we have come to be who we are both as individuals and as members of a wider society.

Studying history sharpens your insights into the functioning of past societies, helping you to formulate a more critical awareness of current problems. In understanding past cultures, and learning to respect the reasoned views of others, students learn the values of tolerance and acceptance of diversity, which are essential today. Furthermore, curiosity informs all historical enquiries and studying history encourages the application of skills of analysis, argument and critical thinking, which are all highly valued in the modern employment market.

# WHAT SKILLS OR ATTRIBUTES DO ADMISSIONS TUTORS LOOK FOR IN A GOOD APPLICANT?

Most of all, admissions tutors are looking for enthusiasm for history; you need to want to steep yourself in the subject for three years. We are particularly looking for candidates who show that their enthusiasm goes far beyond the confines of the curriculum, for example by attending lectures, visiting historical sites, and reading widely in history in their spare time. Equally, we don't want you only to be interested in history: indication of commitment to cultural, sporting, political, or charitable interests is a sign that you are a rounded individual, capable of managing your time and contributing to the community.

# WHAT DOES A GOOD PERSONAL STATEMENT LOOK LIKE?

## Example of a good Personal Statement

I have always been fascinated by history, and am enormously looking forward to the chance to devote myself to the study of different historical periods and problems at university. As part of my A2 studies this year, I have been studying England under the Tudors, a course that I have really enjoyed. I have increased my knowledge and understanding of this course in my own time by attending evening lectures by prominent historians like David Starkey. I have also taken the opportunity to read some recent books providing a broader context to my studies, and have particularly enjoyed Reformation: Europe's House Divided by Diarmaid MacCulloch. My other area of particular historical interest is the Crusades and I have recently been reading God's War: A New History of the Crusades by Christopher Tyerman, which offers a provocative new interpretation of the Crusades. I have also pursued my interest in medieval history by visiting castles on a recent family holiday in Wales, though I am not sure that my younger sister shared my appreciation for the finer points of fortifications!

The other subjects I am studying for A2 level reinforce my interest in history. Sociology helps to provide models for human behaviour, and historians have successfully applied the theories of sociologists like Max Weber to their studies of modern societies. Studying Shakespeare's Richard II for my A2 coursework in English has helped me understand the ideals of kingship that were current during the reign of Elizabeth I.

Outside my schoolwork, I enjoy acting, and recently took the lead role in a school production of West Side Story. I have also been involved in my local branch of Amnesty International, co-ordinating letter-writing campaigns for political prisoners. Fitting in these activities alongside my crowded school schedule has been hard work, but has encouraged me to manage my time effectively. I believe that this balance of work and other activities demonstrates that I will be able to flourish at university.

 **TOP TIPS**

**1** State clearly why you want to study history at university

**2** Give evidence of real enthusiasm for the subject, which goes well beyond the confines of the curriculum

**3** Draw appropriate connections between your chosen subject of history and your other subjects

**4** Show that you have extracurricular interests, to indicate that you are a well-rounded individual who is able to balance various commitments and manage your time effectively

 **THINGS TO AVOID**

**1** Spelling and punctuation errors

**2** Lazy sentence construction and a lack of coherent structure and form

**3** Lies about what you claim to have read and done

**4** Plagiarism

**5** Poor research in the first place, leading to poor decisions: this is often apparent in a statement that lacks evidence that you understand the course and its demands

 **RECOMMENDED READING AND WEBSITES**

- *BBC History Magazine*: www.bbchistorymagazine.com
- *History Today*: www.historytoday.com

I am grateful for the support given to me by the history department at Royal Holloway (www.rhul.ac.uk/history) in the production of this profile. Other highly rated courses include those at the universities of Oxford, Cambridge, King's College, London, York and Durham.

# JOURNALISM

This academic profile is a composite of information provided by admissions tutors at City University, London. The information is useful to all applicants, but some of the advice is pertinent to City in particular.

## SUBJECT OVERVIEW

There are several hundred journalism courses around the country, and they vary enormously. Some courses, such as the BA in Journalism at City University London, have a practical approach, equipping would-be journalists with the core skills they need, including recognising what is newsworthy, researching a story, writing and presentation, whether for the internet, print or broadcast, or all three. Other courses are more theoretical, and are more like media studies courses, with a strong element of communication theory.

Take great care to study course outlines at the various universities you are looking at, to make sure you apply for the kind of course you want. If you are determined to become a journalist, then a more practical course will be more likely to lead to a job. Such a degree, whether as a single or joint honours with another subject such as economics, politics or history, will help towards a job in journalism as well as in related areas such as public relations and event management.

### What journalism is like, and what skills a journalist, or a journalism student, needs

Journalism is good fun, for lots of reasons: It is about **being there** – being outside No 10 for Barack Obama's visit, at Wembley for the cup final, or maybe reporting at the centre of a natural disaster. The subject is about finding out something that no-one else knows, and then telling them (always a fun thing to do). You can carefully craft stories and show them to other people, whether it is in a blog, a glossy magazine, or a TV programme. Journalism is always new and different: the event that has just happened, the story that makes today different from yesterday. No two days are the same for a journalist, and this makes for an exciting life. It might change the world for the better, by bringing important information to the public, for example about a miscarriage of justice.

Journalists do a huge range of different jobs, including reporting, editing copy, writing columns, taking photos, designing for print or web, and putting together broadcast packages for internet sites and/or for radio and TV – so don't think that every journalist is like Jeremy Paxman. Many people think that to be a journalist you need to be an aggressive foot-in-the-door reporter. This is not true. Journalists very rarely operate like that, and in most cases it would be counter-productive if they did. Getting a good story depends far more on building a rapport with your contacts and getting them on your side.

# WHAT SKILLS OR ATTRIBUTES DO ADMISSIONS TUTORS LOOK FOR IN A GOOD APPLICANT?

A good journalist needs to be inquisitive, interested in people, in what is going on, and look into why something has happened, and what its implications are. A journalist needs to have ideas, to be able to think creatively but they also need to be a good listener.

If the university holds interviews, the tutors will certainly ask what papers and magazines you read and what news and current affairs programmes and websites you follow. They might want to know who your favourite journalist is: whose job you would like to have in 10 years' time.

To get on to a journalism course, students need to show that they are creative. This will often be demonstrated by written material and might also include an interest in design and photography. Tutors may expect a potential student to have done some blogging, perhaps about local sport, or music, but any writing would be of interest, from poetry to the first novel.

Attention to detail is very important: although many people believe there are too many errors in newspapers, it is amazing how few there are, considering how much material is edited and put together in such a short time. A good journalist not only needs to know where to put an apostrophe, but needs to **care** that is it is the right place.

## WHAT DOES A GOOD PERSONAL STATEMENT LOOK LIKE?

Your Personal Statement is the only way to show the admissions tutor that you can write well, so spend as much time as possible on it. Make the statement (and yourself) as interesting as possible. Work out what makes you different from the next applicant, and focus on that so that you stand out from the crowd. If you are determined, for example, to be a political journalist, write a bit about what interests you about politics, show that you know what is going on, mention what papers you read, talk about where you would like to work. If it is music that interests you, don't just say you like music – every young person does. Talk about the particular genres that interest you, the particular magazines or websites that you want to write for.

If you are applying to several different types of courses, say perhaps politics at one university, and journalism at another, take care not to be too specific, or you will put off at least one of the admissions tutors.

### Example of a good Personal Statement

The following Personal Statement demonstrates the student's talent for writing. It is well laid out, error-free and punchy. Their work and extracurricular pursuits show their enthusiasm for journalism – something which is essential throughout your career.

> In 2005 I found my first love: music. The influx of new bands and my first live experiences convinced me that I had to work in the industry. As we began to do more creative writing in English, I realised that I wanted to combine these two interests. This gave me an ambition: music journalism. Later, inspired by my work in media studies, I set up an online music fanzine to get my reviews out there.

✓ This is a strong introduction which gives admissions tutors essential information about the student's achievements and ambitions straight away.

June 2008 was a turning point. I was selected to attend The Tony Wilson Experience – a major event, inspiring and offering opportunity to young people through discussion with those experienced in the creative industries. There, I met a writer who offered me the chance to write for award-winning music fanzine, High Voltage. I now regularly contribute reviews and features to the online and print editions. The Manchester Evening News (MEN) City Life (entertainment supplement) editor ran a contest to report on the event. Despite stiff competition, mine was chosen as winner. My work was published and I was able to organise work experience.

During my time at the MEN I had four articles published. It was made even more interesting with the challenge of writing on new subjects, including art exhibitions. I did my first interview, and though nervous at first, thoroughly enjoyed the experience. Since then, contacting people to get unique quotes for articles has been instinctive. My online experience encouraged my editor to involve me in City Life's website launch. Learning about the transition was fascinating and gave me an insight into how the industry is evolving. I now regularly contribute reviews and features to Citylife.co.uk.

✓ This section is important, as it goes into more detail about the student's experience, awards and the recognition that they have received as a result of their own hard work outside of college. The student's passion for journalism, especially within the creative industries, comes through clearly, which is something that we look out for in all our students.

At college I took music technology to gain an understanding of what makes good quality music. Learning about how genres and recording techniques have developed made me think more analytically about music. A desire to gain a wider general knowledge made me take history and critical thinking, but I have learnt a lot about politics and persuasion. I am now better at evidencing my opinions and fascinated by religious practice in early modern Europe, visiting sites around the country to learn more.

English and media studies have given me opportunities to be creative on a range of platforms. I have learnt to write in different styles and found out a lot about communication and media industries. Following my GCSE, I received my school's Media Award for creating an alternative gossip magazine.

✓ You will spend a lot of time doing your A levels, so it good to demonstrate what you have learnt during your studies, even if your A levels are not related to journalism. This student highlights how they have achieved a more in-depth understanding of music through their A level in Music Technology – this supports their ambition of becoming a music journalist as set out at the beginning of the statement.

In my free time I swim and ski to keep fit. The college debating society helps me to explain ideas clearly. Discussing political issues (another major passion) with people of different opinions gives me new ways of looking at things.

I have been playing the guitar for eight years. My tutor, a recording artist, teaches me a lot about the music industry and theory.

> On a trip to Cuba I was captivated by the culture, history and people of Havana. It renewed my childhood interest in the language, so over the summer I took an evening course to gain a basic level of Spanish.
>
> Following volunteer work at a Plaza Theatre, I joined the Youth Action Team. Together, we promote volunteering to young people and develop new opportunities for them.

✓ Talking about your extracurricular activities, like this student, demonstrates that you are a rounded person who can manage their time. University life is busy, so the ability to balance your studies, socialising, volunteering or work experience is a key skill to have.

 **TOP TIPS**

**1** Remember you are applying to a course that is all about the written word: your statement should be concise, clear and written in a vibrant style

**2** Give examples of writing you have done thus far: if you have edited a school magazine, we want to know

**3** Talk about your skills and how you have acquired them

**4** Talk about your extracurricular pursuits, particularly those where you need initiative and drive to succeed: hard work is commendable!

 **THINGS TO AVOID**

**1** Poor spelling, grammar and punctuation: get the statement proofread by someone competent to spot these errors

**2** Plagiarism: the worst sin, as this is a profession that relies on creative writing, not copying others' ideas and passing them off as your own

**3** Saying anything that you could not justify or explain at interview: many courses do interview now, as competition for places is high

**4** Underselling your achievements: universities want confident go-getters, not those who hide their lights under bushels

 **RECOMMENDED READING AND WEBSITES**

- Emma Caprez, *Careers Uncovered: Journalism*, 2nd edition, Trotman Publishing, 2009
- Anna McKane, *Journalism: A Career Handbook*, A&C Black, 2004

I am grateful to City for providing the information used to prepare this profile. Other highly rated courses include those at the universities of Cardiff, University of the Arts London, Anglia Ruskin and Bournemouth.

# LAW

**This academic profile was written by admissions tutors at City University London and focuses on law as a single honours discipline. The information contained within is useful to all applicants, but please be aware that some of the advice is pertinent to the City Law School in particular.**

## SUBJECT OVERVIEW

A career in the legal profession is not only personally rewarding, interesting and challenging, but it can also be lucrative. Law is a dynamic, fast-changing subject to study. Of course there is a great deal of acquisition of knowledge involved, but the most important aspect of studying law is the application of that knowledge. It is part science, part language and part art, so students from a wide range of academic backgrounds may find that it suits them.

The skills gained by a law student are popular with employers across many fields, allowing students to take their skills into many other professions. A good law student will be able to research, negotiate, debate, persuade, apply theory, have logical thought processes and present themselves well in writing and in person, all of which skills are readily transferable to graduate employment.

## WHAT SKILLS OR ATTRIBUTES DO ADMISSIONS TUTORS LOOK FOR IN A GOOD APPLICANT?

There are no specific subjects requirements for law (at undergraduate level any combination can work very well). We do normally expect candidates' subjects to be broadly academic. There are however, a few core skills that make a good candidate. These include excellent written and oral communication, logical reasoning and problem solving, and the ability to search out information and question your findings.

The best law students are able to see all viewpoints on a factual scenario, discuss them in a balanced fashion, then argue each and every one of them as if it was the only possible perspective. They will have, or acquire, the ability to solve problems, since that is largely what lawyers are paid to do. They will show a high level of accuracy and care in their written work, since the lack of either can have truly disastrous consequences in law.

Intending law students are expected to demonstrate that they are committed to studying at degree level, and committed to studying law in particular. Most law degrees require a very strong academic record, but that is not enough; a genuine enthusiasm for the subject will also go a long way. Simply saying that you really want to study law will not do: you need to prove it, so mention any work experience or other extracurricular activities that demonstrate your passion for law.

Not all good lawyers or law students are naturally confident, and too much confidence can lead to sloppy preparation. There is no such thing as a lawyer who does not interact with other people at all, so those on the shy side of humanity need to be prepared to give presentations and participate in mock trials, once they are at university.

## WHAT DOES A GOOD PERSONAL STATEMENT LOOK LIKE?

Think about your target audience – the admissions tutor. That person's job is to try and work out whether or not you will perform well on their course.

A strong academic background is not enough in itself; you need to show that you are entering the right degree for you. Show that a) you know a little about the subject and b) you really want to study it. You might be able to use evidence of additional work or reading in the area, but be careful about how you demonstrate your passion and knowledge of the subject. Watching a lot of television shows about law is unlikely to impress admissions tutors, but making the effort to go to courts and watch trials is far more relevant.

If you want to study law, your Personal Statement needs to be polished, without grammatical or typographical errors. Remember that accuracy and presentation are very important in law. It is generally a highly competitive field, so it is best not to provide any grounds for rejecting your application. Meeting the standard offer for your chosen course is not enough, since there will be hundreds of other applicants with identical predicted grades. Your application needs to stand out (in a good way!).

Think carefully about how you can highlight the core skills and attributes needed, including problem-solving, academic dedication, logical thinking and the ability to argue persuasively. You may have some directly relevant work experience, but you may find examples in more surprising places.

## Example of a good Personal Statement

I have visited Harrow Crown Court on several occasions to broaden my perspective of the legal system. The most remarkable case I watched was a case against a police officer who was charged with conspiracy. I witnessed the jury's importance and their deliberation process, the judge's authority in the courtroom and received a general idea of how the trials are conducted.

✓ This shows the candidate's strong interest in the subject which they have demonstrated well by discussing specific trials.

A level Law has given me a deeper understanding of legal principles, whilst the study of politics and international relations gave me a greater insight as to where the law can be applied. I decided to study mathematics, because it is essential for improvement of logistics. History, law and politics developed my critical and analytical skills.

✓ Explaining your choices of A level subjects is good, particularly if you can emphasise the skills developed during these courses, and their relevance to law. These skills are important since they take time to develop.

In February 2005, I took part in Model United Nations conference in Italy, where young mentors all around the world tried to find a resolution to global problems. It helped me to develop my debating skills and public speaking as well as research and negotiation skills. I will be attending the MUN in 2007.

✓ This shows an interest in the subject and commitments to extracurricular activities, and also demonstrates that the candidate recognises and has skills needed to study law. The candidate also demonstrates key skills needed for law – problem solving, debating an issue and public speaking.

> For my work experience I was interviewed and was successful in gaining a work placement in Varley, Hadley and Siddall criminal law solicitors firm in Nottingham. In the week that followed I was able to shadow qualified solicitors, help with office work and view various trials and cases in both Crown and magistrate's courts.

✓ This candidate has tried to improve their experience of law by taking a work experience placement, which shows dedication to the subject.

> During my high school years I was awarded the honour of becoming a prefect, which gave me the responsibility of maintaining an orderly environment and setting an example. I also helped arrange my school boat trip, which allowed me to develop my organisation and leadership qualities.

✓ Organisation skills and a responsible mature attitude are very important for studying law, as you will be expected to do a lot of studying and extra reading in your own time.

 ## TOP TIPS

**1** Give evidence for all of your assertions about your abilities and suitability for a law degree. Keep the evidence specific rather than making general claims about always having wanted to be a lawyer

**2** Do your research about the details of the courses you have selected, and make sure that what you say fits them. If the university does not enter moots, telling them how you are drawn to their mooting programme will not impress the admissions tutor; if they do not run a competition law module, indicating that you are keen to study it may puzzle

 ## THINGS TO AVOID

**1** Do not say anything inaccurate or embellished: you are likely to be caught out if there is an interview, or worse, once you have started a course. Accuracy and ethics are very important in law

**2** It is wise not to assume that having studied law at A level will give you a great advantage. Some students who have done so, do find it very helpful, but there is a large gap between A level law and degree level law, and it is very dangerous to think that you can simply rely on existing notes and knowledge without doing a great deal of extra work. Some universities

the tutor and looks like poor research

**3** Check your form (repeatedly) for errors: do not use words which you cannot spell

do not count A level law for admissions purposes

---

# RECOMMENDED READING AND WEBSITES

- Phil Harris, *An Introduction to Law*, Cambridge University Press, 2006
- Catherine Elliott and Frances Quinn, *English Legal System*; Longman, 2007
- Carl Lygo, *Getting Into Law*, 8th edition, Trotman Publishing, 2010
- Clare Rhoden and Simon Chesterman, *Studying Law at University: Everything You Need to Know*, Allen & Unwin, 2005

I am grateful for the support of City University School of Law in writing this profile. Other highly rated courses can be found at the universities of Birmingham, UCL, LSE, Cambridge and Edinburgh.

# MATHEMATICS

This academic profile was written by an admissions tutor at Royal Holloway, University of London. The information in this profile is useful to all applicants, but some of the advice is pertinent to that department in particular.

## SUBJECT OVERVIEW

For some, mathematics is a pure science to be studied for its intrinsic beauty and logical structure. For many it means problem solving and the satisfaction of getting what is indisputably the 'right' answer. Others will consider the myriad and diverse applications of mathematics, in areas such as finance or quantum information. The truth is that mathematics encompasses all these and more, because each perspective is fundamentally linked to the others.

By studying mathematics you gain a diverse range of transferable skills, including how to apply a universal language in a multiplicity of situations and see connections between them. Mathematics also provides an excellent foundation for a variety of fulfilling career paths or opportunities for further study.

## WHAT SKILLS OR ATTRIBUTES DO ADMISSIONS TUTORS LOOK FOR IN A GOOD APPLICANT?

The three things that interest us most are: mathematics, mathematics and mathematics! That is perhaps an over-simplification, but your mathematical talent is by far the most important factor for admissions tutors. Of course, they are also looking for an enthusiasm that will sustain you over three or four years. University study is more independent than at school, so that time management skills, determination to succeed, and a good work ethic are also highly relevant. Evidence of social activities undertaken in your spare time is also useful.

## WHAT DOES A GOOD PERSONAL STATEMENT LOOK LIKE?

A good Personal Statement is, above all, personal. It gives you the chance to speak directly to the admissions tutor about yourself, your reasons for choosing a particular degree programme, your choice of A level subjects, your personal interests and out-of-school activities; in summary, what makes you tick.

Be honest: if you say that a particular branch of mathematics interests you, or you have read a particular book, then this is likely to be a topic of discussion at interview. Talk about your current skills and attributes, particularly if they are either mathematical (you might like puzzles, chess, strategy games) or non-academic (such as leadership, initiative or examples of personal challenges that you have overcome). Include anything that you would like the admissions tutor to know about you that would not be covered elsewhere on the form.

 **TOP TIPS**

**1** Your statement should be clear, concise and free from errors

**2** Your statement should explain clearly in the opening paragraph why maths is your choice of degree and, more importantly, what evidence you can provide that supports this view

**3** Mention it if you have obtained high scores in tests or taken part in national maths challenges

**4** Mention your non-academic attributes, too: leadership, personal success in tasks and any work experience or taster courses

**5** Mention if you have a career in mind that lends itself to maths

 **THINGS TO AVOID**

**1** Spelling and other mistakes

**2** Poorly constructed sentences that do not follow logically

**3** Underemphasising your skills and why they will be suitable for maths

**4** Not mentioning your work ethic and attitude to individual learning

**5** Appearing to be unsociable and unwilling to engage in extracurricular pursuits

 **RECOMMENDED READING AND WEBSITES**

- Tom Körner, *The Pleasures of Counting*, Cambridge University Press, 1996. This uses examples as diverse as the outbreak of cholera in Victorian Soho, the Battle of the Atlantic, African Eve, and the design of anchors to show the kind of problems that interest mathematicians and the kind of ways in which they attack them

I am grateful for the support I received from the maths department at Royal Holloway (www.ma.rhul.ac.uk) in the preparation of this profile. Other highly rated courses include those at the universities of Cambridge, Oxford, Warwick, Greenwich and Leicester.

# MEDICINE

This academic profile was written by an admissions tutor at Brighton and Sussex Medical School. The information is useful to all applicants, but some of the advice is pertinent to BSMS in particular.

UCAS permits you to apply to a maximum of four medical schools. Given the competition for places, it is imperative that you use all of your application slots. I recommend that you also apply for an alternative course in your fifth slot, with biomedical science, biochemistry and neuroscience being ideal alternatives. This way you may, should you gain a good degree, be able to enter medical school via one of the popular graduate entry schemes. Applicants without the required academic profile may find it possible to gain entry to one of the foundation courses, where a student is admitted to medical school after they complete a foundation year.

## SUBJECT OVERVIEW

Becoming a doctor isn't an easy option – it takes years of study and hard work. As you learn the skills you need, you will also learn a great deal about yourself. If you like helping people there are few more rewarding or respected careers. You'll be part of a team of professionals and non-medical staff delivering care to the highest standards in the NHS. Medicine is about helping people – treating illness, providing advice and reassurance, and seeing the effects of both ill health and good health from the patient's point of view. You have to examine the symptoms presented by a patient, and consider a range of possible diagnoses of their cause. You must test your diagnosis, decide on the best course of treatment, and monitor progress. This demands an enquiring mind, the capacity to acquire and maintain high levels of knowledge that have to be constantly up to date, and the ability to relate to people as individuals each with their own health needs.

If you have that passion to improve people's lives and the determination to reach the highest standards, you will have many career opportunities. You can follow a path to one of many specialisms, from working in a hospital as a surgeon to being based in the community as a GP. The training and support available to you in the NHS can help you get to the very top of your chosen career.

Medicine is a demanding profession, but one that repays the hard work and dedication it involves through the rich variety of career opportunities it offers. Whether helping patients, managing a hospital or pushing back the borders of medical research, you will have the satisfaction of knowing that you are making a positive contribution to society.

At university, you will be kept busy with a mixture of seminars, lectures, anatomy classes, clinical skills practice and patient interaction, depending on where you study. In later years you will spend more time with medical teams than in the classroom. Assessments may be through exams, written portfolios or practical tests. Medical students are also known for their busy social lives!

## WHAT SKILLS OR ATTRIBUTES DO ADMISSIONS TUTORS LOOK FOR IN A GOOD APPLICANT?

You will need the ability, the commitment and the personal qualities necessary to become an excellent doctor. Academically, BSMS requires 340 UCAS points at A level, including an A in Biology or Chemistry at AS level. Many equivalent qualifications are accepted, depending on whether you have studied abroad, or already completed a degree. Most medical schools also require you to take the UK Clinical Aptitude Test (UKCAT: www.ukcat.ac.uk) or Biomedical Admissions Test (BMAT: www.admissionstests.cambridgeassessment.org.uk/adt/bmat).

Just as important are a realistic attitude to medical training and clinical practice, a commitment to caring for others, the ability to communicate and work effectively within a team and to appreciate other people's points of view, and a willingness to accept responsibility.

## WHAT DOES A GOOD PERSONAL STATEMENT LOOK LIKE?

Medicine is a diverse profession with specialisms that suit a wide range of people. We want our student body to reflect the variety of the profession and of society as a whole, and are not looking for any one model of Personal Statement.

Your Personal Statement should contain a short introduction about why you want to study medicine. Indicate what relevant experience you have, perhaps with a GP, in a hospital, hospice, care home or with disabled groups, and how you have reflected on and learned from it. This work experience is hard to achieve but the fact that you have will tell us that you have the drive and passion to succeed.

Do let us know what you learnt from the work experience rather than just telling us what you did. The tutor will be looking for evidence that you know what it is like to be a doctor and know a bit about healthcare practice. We need to weed out those who think it is like *ER* or *Holby City*!

Demonstrate your understanding of scientific and medical issues; regular reading will help. I suggest that you read quite widely, particularly in the lead up to your interview. You ought to be aware of issues in medicine that you will have heard discussed in broadsheet newspapers and scientific journals.

Include not only what you have learned through study but your other activities and non-academic achievements – sports, hobbies, travel, awards and so on. Show what relevant qualities you have developed from your experiences, for example in communicating, leadership or teamwork.

Avoid poor spelling, grammar and punctuation. This leaves a poor impression and, while not hugely significant, you cannot really afford to be seen as careless when competition is so fierce.

**TOP TIPS**

**1** Find out as much as you can about what it is like to be a doctor. Talk to healthcare professionals, read as much as you can and get some relevant work experience. Mention what you have learnt as a result in the statement and be willing to discuss it at interview

**2** Research the prospectuses and websites of a variety of medical schools, and visit some to make sure you find the course, teaching styles, facilities and location that are right for you. When you start your statement, it might be worth mentioning the fact that you have done this and the choices you have made reflect your interests and learning styles

**3** Begin work on your Personal Statement early: the UCAS deadline for medicine courses is earlier than for other university programmes. Get comments from other people and write several drafts. Make sure you are happy with it before you submit it to UCAS

**4** Read the BMA's excellent guide *Becoming a Doctor*, which you can download at the BMA website www.bma.org.uk. The advice there will help you construct a good statement and prepare for the interview

 **THINGS TO AVOID**

**1** Making any claims in your Personal Statement that you cannot substantiate at interview

**2** Plagiarising any part of your Personal Statement: when admissions tutors read through over 2,000 applications, this soon becomes obvious

**3** Taking an inflexible stance on contentious issues: you need to be able to work with people who hold all kinds of opinions

**4** Memorising set answers to the interview questions you think you might get: the interviewers will be able to get to know you better through a natural conversation

**5** Going into medicine because other people want you to: don't succumb to their pressure if you don't feel it's the right choice for you

# RECOMMENDED READING AND WEBSITES

- Steven Piumatti, *Getting Into Medical School 2011 Entry*, 15th edition, Richmond: Trotman Publishing, 2010
- *Becoming a Doctor*, BMA website: www.bma.org.uk
- General Medical Council: www.gmc-uk.org
- Tomorrow's Doctors on the GMC website: www.gmc-uk.org/education/ undergraduate/undergraduate_policy/tomorrows_doctors.asp
- Want to be a Doctor website: www.wanttobeadoctor.co.uk A fantastic site that provides great advice about applications to this competitive course

I am grateful to the Brighton and Sussex Medical School (www.bsms.ac.uk) for their help in preparing this profile.

# MIDWIFERY

This academic profile was written by an admissions tutor at Swansea University. The information in this profile is useful to all applicants, but some of the advice is pertinent to Swansea in particular.

## SUBJECT OVERVIEW

Midwives offer individual care to women and their families and help them take part in their own care planning during pregnancy. Both during and after pregnancy you will be with the new mother in her own locality.

Midwifery is as much about supporting the new mother and her partner, as helping with the birth of the baby. Support continues from the confirmation of the pregnancy through to the postnatal days after the baby is born.

The philosophy of a degree course in midwifery is to prepare a midwife who is able to practise at the point of registration. It is designed to build upon an individual's strengths and to value her life experiences to develop into a professional and motivated practitioner. Students develop a heightened level of self-awareness and sensitivity towards women and families throughout the programme.

The learner is expected to grow in confidence and self-awareness, to take responsibility for their personal and professional development. Students then emerge into the practice arena as lifelong learners – confident, competent and accountable for their own practice as a midwife meeting the challenges of contemporary practice.

The new graduate will get to see the miracle of new life on a daily basis. From measuring pregnancy bumps to taking command during labour, hearing the first squawk of a new arrival and then visiting them during their first few weeks – most midwives say they couldn't have a more satisfying job! However, the hours are tough and the pay isn't fantastic, especially when you consider how important experts in this field are. At degree level students of midwifery get frontline and academic experience of how to lead women and babies through such a crucial stage of life.

## WHAT SKILLS OR ATTRIBUTES DO ADMISSIONS TUTORS LOOK FOR IN A GOOD APPLICANT?

Candidates need to be caring and understanding individuals with a sensitive nature. Good communication skills are essential in this career. Most midwives are committed, extremely motivated and usually female. Being unsqueamish, staunchly practical and having a no-nonsense attitude is a must.

Most candidates in the UK who wish to enter the degree programme at Swansea must have achieved three A levels at grade C or above (two AS levels = one A level), or a score of 240 tariff points (or equivalent), plus English/Welsh language, maths and a science at GCSE grade C or above. All students must be able to demonstrate key skills and numeracy. These requirements will vary between institutions. At the top end, King's College, London asks for BBC at

A level. You'll need a clean Criminal Records Bureau disclosure and occupational health clearance to get into any course in the UK.

Departments across the UK welcome applications from students of all ages including mature students who have evidence of recent appropriate study (within the last five years) and with alternative qualifications such as Access to higher education programmes.

Swansea, like most university departments, treats all applications for admission on their individual merits and welcomes applications from candidates with a range of qualifications.

Many departments, including Swansea, due to the competition for a small number of places, cannot consider applications for deferred entry. You should also expect to be interviewed by most departments. They will expect a candidate to have a good working knowledge of the profession and issues relating to the profession.

## WHAT DOES A GOOD PERSONAL STATEMENT LOOK LIKE?

You should write convincingly about your clear understanding of the role of the midwife and how your experience and attributes fit well with a career in midwifery. You should research demands of the role and current NHS practice so that you can demonstrate your awareness of the role in the opening part of the statement, and show that you understand that midwives work with people from all walks of life and often in stressful situations. This may, but does not have to, involve some work experience or personal contact with a practising midwife.

We like to see evidence of the key skills required, both academic and non-academic, and would like to hear what particular skills you have developed in your A level or equivalent studies. The sciences are important to emphasise but we do also look for breadth – make sure that you know the academic demands of each department you apply to before writing your statement. We also look for clarity, good spelling and grammar and evidence that you are involved in a wide range of extracurricular pursuits.

**TOP TIPS**

**1** Do all that you can to access information to lead you to really understand the rigours of a career in midwifery and the demands of a three-year midwifery degree

**2** Be prepared to explain all of this in your statement and in the interview

**3** Show us that you have the academic potential to cope with the demands of the subject, by alluding to these skills in your statement

 **THINGS TO AVOID**

**1** Referring too much to your own birth experiences (if you have any)

**2** Applying to become a midwife if your real interest lies in caring for babies and children

**3** Spelling, punctuation and grammar mistakes: make sure that your statement is read carefully by another person before you submit it. Check that the spell check is set to UK as default

---

 **RECOMMENDED READING AND WEBSITES**

- Laurel Alexander, *Careers Uncovered: Nursing and Midwifery*, 2nd edition, Trotman Publishing, 2006
- Penny Armstrong and Sheryl Fieldman, *A Midwife's Story*, Pinter & Martin, 2006
- Stella McKay Moffat and Pamela Lee, *A Pocket Guide for Student Midwives*, Wiley Blackwell, 2006
- The Nursing and Midwifery Council: www.nmc-uk.org
- Royal College of Nursing: www.rcn.org.uk

I am grateful to the midwifery department at Swansea University (www.swan. ac.uk/ugcourses/HealthScience/BMidMidwifery) for their support in preparing this profile. Other highly rated courses can be found at the universities of Sheffield Hallam, Glasgow Caledonian, Leeds, Manchester and King's College, London.

# MODERN LANGUAGES

This academic profile was written with the help of the Universities of Surrey and Birmingham. The information is useful to all applicants, but some of the advice is pertinent to those departments in particular.

## SUBJECT OVERVIEW

Modern language courses in the UK tend towards the languages that are studied in most UK schools, namely French, German, Spanish and Italian. They can be studied as a single subject or as part of a joint honours degree. Popular combinations include modern languages with business, politics, economics, media studies, law and history. Other languages on offer in UK universities include Russian, Arabic, Hebrew, Mandarin, Japanese, Portuguese, Greek (modern) and the Nordic languages.

If you study single honours you will concentrate on one subject for all four years. In your first two years you will also often take one module chosen from a wide range across the university, but apart from that your studies will be devoted to a single subject. For combinations of two languages, you would normally apply to read a BA in Modern Languages. In joint honours programmes you will study one modern language equally weighted with another subject that is not a modern language.

Spending a year abroad is a common element of language courses. This can be extremely beneficial, as immersing yourself in a language as a resident of that country extends your knowledge significantly. This option is not cheap so bear that in mind when you apply.

## WHAT SKILLS OR ATTRIBUTES DO ADMISSIONS TUTORS LOOK FOR IN A GOOD APPLICANT?

Usually the entry requirements are largely self-evident, in that you need a language to A level (or equivalent), but some courses allow you to start a language from the beginning. In fact, you can do pretty much all the languages from beginner level (sometimes called *ab initio*) – apart from French at Birmingham – but only in particular combinations.

For instance, if you're doing two modern languages you need to have one to A level, but you could start the other from beginner level. This is a common feature of many courses in the UK. For example, you might have German to A level, but you want to pick up Italian or Portuguese from scratch. You obviously wouldn't be able to start a single honours language course such as German studies from beginner level, though. You would need an A level in that language. It is distinctions like these that are important to note, and it shows why the research in advance is so vital. Every year about 5% of our applicants apply for courses for which they don't have the requisite qualifications and waste a choice on their UCAS forms. In a lot of cases it's because they have not done enough research before they complete their UCAS form.

Non-academic traits include a sound mind, an evident zest for life and an interest in languages and cultures. We need to see some evidence of this when we read a Personal Statement or interview a candidate.

## WHAT DOES A GOOD PERSONAL STATEMENT LOOK LIKE?

Over the past four to five years, school teachers have become more aware that it is increasingly competitive, and they need to give more help and support to applicants with getting their Personal Statements right. What this seems to have done is create quite a number of 'template' Personal Statements that all look very much like each other. One of the things tutors recommend is to go for something a little different, without being idiosyncratic. Punctuation and grammar are also vital, especially if the course is competitive.

If you say you're interested in languages, the university wants to know why you're interested in the course. What sparked that interest? What have you done to show that interest in a real way? For example, if you've been doing extra reading around the A level curriculum, write it down. Refer to books or magazines that you have read in the native language. Mention foreign travel, exchanges that you have been on or any other pertinent information that supports your case. If you are already bilingual, say so. It will give an indication that you have a talent for languages, even if the languages that you speak are not those that you hope to read.

Tutors are also looking for applicants who are likely to adapt to the university way of thinking. They are looking for a critical mindset, for students who will be enquiring and analytical, and willing to get involved in intellectual debate. They like those who can convey that sense of excitement at getting involved in an intellectual debate.

## Example of a good Personal Statement

> My decision to study French and Spanish stems not only from a genuine desire to further my knowledge, but also because of the experiences I have already had through using foreign languages.

✓ Relates past positive reactions of language learning to future chosen course of study.

> I have chosen to study French because I am passionate about language learning. In my French studies I particular enjoy learning about French culture. One topic I found particularly interesting was 'Immigration and Multiculturalism' and how successfully north African immigrants, for instance, are integrated into French society.

✓ Shows openness to other cultures, multicultural perspectives.

> Through studying Spanish at A level I have learnt a great deal about the history of Spain, with topics such as the Spanish Civil War and the reign of Franco. I am also fascinated by Spanish culture and have learnt about the architecture of Gaudi and the art of the Flamenco.

✓ Awareness of how political and cultural influences shape language study.

> During my German studies I went on a 5-day trip to Strasbourg, Freiburg and Baden Baden. A visit to the European Parliament – where the best interpreters and translators work – has given me a good insight into what an interpreter's career entails.

✓ Concrete evidence of unearthing vocational applications of languages.

## TOP TIPS

**1** Think hard about what you want to do before you start to write your Personal Statement

**2** Think about what you enjoy and what you love and express this in your statement

**3** If you are applying for a language, tutors need to know that you have the aptitude to succeed. Mention in your statement your current level of fluency, the experience you have of speaking the language with native speakers and any exchange trip you may have been involved with

**4** Make sure that your Personal Statement is clear, concise, free from basic errors and sells you in a compelling manner

## THINGS TO AVOID

**1** Lying on your Personal Statement: lies are often found out and this can lead to the reject bin or worse!

**2** Plagiarising from another statement: be inspired by exemplars but ultimately be yourself! UCAS checks Personal Statements for signs of plagiarism and informs that university if they are suspicious

**3** Spelling, punctuation and grammar errors on your statement: this is just lazy

**4** Applying before you have done the right research: check the entry requirements and make sure that the course on offer plays to your strengths

**5** Glib, generalised comments: they often irritate. It is a professional document and the language should be professional in tone, not too conversational or text speak-like!

## RECOMMENDED READING AND WEBSITES

■ You should read a range of different publications in the language you wish to study – newspapers, magazines (both serious and glossy), books and even comic books

I would like to acknowledge the support of the University of Surrey (www.surrey.ac.uk) and the University of Birmingham (www.bham.ac.uk) in producing this profile. Other highly rated courses can be found at the universities of Oxford, Cambridge, UCL, Bath and Southampton.

# MUSIC

**This academic profile was written by admissions tutors at Southampton University. The information is useful to all applicants, but some of the advice is pertinent to that department in particular.**

**At this point I would like to point out that you could also, if you think it is appropriate for you, apply to read music at one of the conservatoires. These are specialist music colleges with a strong emphasis on musical performance, conducting and composition. A very high level of musical aptitude is expected. Applications are made direct to the conservatoire or via the CUKAS system (see Chapter Ten).**

## SUBJECT OVERVIEW

Studying music at university is like Christmas coming early all the year round. Everyone who contemplates a music degree will have been bitten by the music bug from an early age, and will have been spending most of their free time at school developing instrumental and vocal skills, learning about music and how to write it, and participating in ensembles from garage bands to symphony orchestras. At university, you get to continue this passion, except that you get to do it full time. There is no subject on offer at university with such a clear match between reality and your ambitions.

From your first day at university, you'll be engaged in understanding how music works and translating that understanding into the performances you want to give. You'll be taught by experts in your field and given lots of opportunities to display your knowledge in public performances in front of your peers and the rest of the community.

Career prospects for music graduates are excellent, since they are equipped with the crucial qualities of communication and self-expression, interaction and teamwork, and time management. Our graduates go on to careers in teaching, media, arts administration, performance, composition, journalism, production and sound engineering, and postgraduate study.

## WHAT SKILLS OR ATTRIBUTES DO ADMISSIONS TUTORS LOOK FOR IN A GOOD APPLICANT?

Universities look for applicants with excellent A level results and with experience and abilities outside their A level curriculum. But a good applicant will also have a sustained profile in instrumental and vocal performance (any style or genre) with evidence of an ability to perform in public both as a soloist and as an ensemble player. This means you have to be an extrovert soloist but at the same time a team player able to work with your colleagues.

## WHAT DOES A GOOD PERSONAL STATEMENT LOOK LIKE?

Be specific about your skills and experiences. What instruments do you play and to what level? Who have you studied with? What ensembles are you part of, and how long have you been a member? How does the practical work tie in with your A level academic work? Give clear indications as why you have chosen this type of institution for your degree, and make clear that you understand how these programmes match your ambitions. What do you do outside of music? In addition, the usual advice applies. Make sure that it is concise, precise and sells you skills well. Avoid spelling and punctuation errors and do not attempt to plagiarise material. This is both fraudulent and easily spotted at interview.

 **TOP TIPS**

**1** Show that you have made a personal investment in music beyond school and make this clear in the body of your Personal Statement

 **THINGS TO AVOID**

**1** Being a specialist who only plays and listens to one kind of music – you need to be receptive to many musical styles and approaches to studying music to

**2** Convince the tutors that you have a genuine interest in *understanding* music, and not just listening to it or performing it

**3** Find out about the specific content of each university's course, and think carefully about which one best matches your interest: a candidate who has taken the trouble to research what's on offer and is really enthused by it will come across well. This research will be evident in your statement

**4** Show that you have a real understanding of what it is like to study music at university, and show that your experiences so far have prepared you for or encouraged you towards a music degree

**5** Don't play down your other strengths and interests: tutors are looking for students who excel not just in music, but have performed well across their school curriculum. Ideally, give some thought to how your study of maths or English or media or whatever has enhanced your appreciation of music!

succeed in a music degree

**2** A statement that is poorly written in terms of style and design. It should be treated as a very important document and be given the time and effort that it deserves

**3** Writing what you think universities want to hear if it is not you. The real you will study at university and a false impression given in the statement will only hinder you in the long term

 ## RECOMMENDED READING AND WEBSITES

▄ Dee Pilgrim, *Careers Uncovered: Performing Arts*, 2nd edition Trotman Publishing, 2007

I am grateful to the Music department at Southampton (www.soton.ac.uk/music), for their assistance in writing this profile. Other highly rated courses can be found at Birmingham, Bristol, Cambridge, Nottingham and King's College, London.

# NURSING

**This academic profile was written by admissions tutors at Swansea University. They can be contacted at www.swan.ac.uk/health_science. For details of all nursing courses you are directed to the UCAS course search facility that lists all the courses on offer in UK institutions. The information in this profile is useful to all applicants, but please be aware that some of the advice is pertinent to that department in particular.**

## SUBJECT OVERVIEW

Nursing is a unique occupation and offers you a chance to help others when they need it most. There has never been a more exciting time to join the nursing profession. Nurses are crucial members of the multi-professional health care team. Furthermore, the number and variety of nursing roles is extensive. Once qualified as a registered nurse you will have opportunities to work in a range of environments including NHS and independent hospitals, GP surgeries, clinics, nursing and residential homes, occupational health services, voluntary organisations, armed forces and industry. Today there are greater opportunities for nurses to take increased responsibility for patient care and to become specialists and advanced practitioners in many areas; for example, intensive care, cancer care and mental health.

## WHAT SKILLS OR ATTRIBUTES DO ADMISSIONS TUTORS LOOK FOR IN A GOOD APPLICANT?

Candidates need the desire to help people. You have to be a practical individual and know how to manage your time. You will, as a nurse, develop effective communication skills and the ability to work in a team, but also act as a leader.

Candidates need to demonstrate a strong educational profile and a clear commitment to their chosen branch of nursing. GCSE profile needs to include English Language, Maths and Science at grades A to C. Candidates usually require a minimum of 240 UCAS tariff points at A level (typically CCC) or equivalent.

- A/AS levels: combination must include two A2 grades
- BTEC National Diploma Health Studies: MMM
- BTEC Higher Diploma Health Science: pass
- Access to Health/Nursing/Science: this should be passed with all core subjects and a minimum of six passes, 33 merits and six distinctions.

All applicants need to demonstrate success at study in the previous three to five years. Although no specific subjects are required, it is beneficial to study health- or science-related courses. Also, care experience may be beneficial.

**Literacy:** applicants are required to demonstrate evidence of ability to read and comprehend in English or Welsh and to communicate effectively in writing. As part of the interview process, applicants are required to write a brief essay.

**Numeracy:** applicants need to demonstrate competency in numeracy in a short test during the interview day.

From November 2010 onwards all students starting their programme will be legally required to register with the Vetting and Barring System (VBS) which is administered by the Independent Safeguarding Authority (www.isa-gov.org.uk). Registration with the scheme will cost £64.00. This is a one-off payment which will cover both the cost of registration and an enhanced Criminal Records Bureau (CRB) check. Following successful registration with the Independent Safeguarding Authority, you will be issued with a unique registration number which will stay with you for the rest of your career. Where programmes require engagement in regulated activity the university is legally required to check applicants' ISA registration.

Therefore, any offer of a place will require:

- Criminal Records Bureau: a police check under the Rehabilitation of Offenders Act (enhanced check required)
- Individual Safeguarding Authority registration

■ Occupational health check: all students are required to adhere to the School of Health Science's vaccination policy unless they are medically exempt.

## WHAT DOES A GOOD PERSONAL STATEMENT LOOK LIKE?

It is helpful if the applicant could talk about the skills they have developed and demonstrate how these skills may be transferable to nursing; for example, skills in communication, team working, organisation, information technology and leadership. The applicant would also be well advised to be able to justify why they have decided to apply for a particular branch of nursing and to highlight any particular interpersonal skills and positions of responsibility held. It may also be helpful for the applicant to show how subjects studied at A level may be applicable to nursing. If the applicant has care experience they may wish to convey what has been learnt from this experience.

### What is the interview process like?

The admission requirements for the pre-registration nursing programme embrace and maintain the standards and professional requirements for pre-registration nurse education while taking account of the current climate in higher education, and embracing the principles of widening access, social inclusion and increasing flexibility.

At Swansea the interview takes place over a morning or afternoon and begins with a short talk to a group of applicants from the admissions tutor. Applicants are then required to complete a short essay and numeracy test before the actual interview. The interview is conducted by two individuals, a member of the School of Health Science's academic staff and a senior nurse from clinical practice. Processes are in place for the conduct of the interviews and criteria employed. The process may be different at other universities.

All applicants are encouraged to prepare for the interview in advance. Good preparation might include: visiting the website for information on the numeracy test, participating in a mock interview and receiving feedback, reading around broad issues relating to nursing and health care, and ensuring familiarity with the Personal Statement.

**TOP TIPS**

**1** Attend careers fairs, university open days and/or arrange to speak with admissions tutors. In addition visit the university or departmental website: you will find information here about the admissions process and the programme. This research is important to reflect in your statement and application

**2** Ensure there are no errors of spelling or grammar in your application and check that details are correct

**3** Ensure that what you write in your Personal Statement is clearly expressed and establishes early on your motivation and commitment to study

**4** Find out about what nurses do: talk to nurses about the profession, health care and nursing roles. Make sure that you reflect this contact in your statement. In addition, keep abreast of topical health care or health-related issues; for example, infection control, nurse prescribing, obesity, health policy – you may be asked about current issues at interview

**5** Prepare for some of the things that you would like to say during the interview. Remind yourself of your Personal Statement before you arrive for any interview –

 **THINGS TO AVOID**

**1** Do not submit a poorly presented UCAS application or statement. There is no excuse for poor spelling or basic punctuation mistakes

**2** Using text-speak in your application, particularly your Personal Statement. This is a professional document and the tone should be professional too

**3** Failing to mention any work experience or contact with health care professionals that you have completed

**4** Appearing to be under-prepared to discuss at interview any material that you have mentioned in the statement or elsewhere in your application your interviewers may ask you about aspects of this. During the interview, if you do not know the meaning of a question, or if you do not know the answer to a question, say so

## RECOMMENDED READING AND WEBSITES

- Laurel Alexander, *Careers Uncovered: Nursing and Midwifery*, 2nd edition, Trotman Publishing, 2006
- The Nursing and Midwifery Council: www.nmc-uk.org
- Royal College of Nursing: www.rcn.org.uk

I am grateful for the support I received from the nursing department at Swansea University (www.swansea.ac.uk) in the preparation of this profile. Other highly regarded courses can be found at the universities of Edinburgh, Liverpool, King's College, London, UEA and Brighton.

# OCEANOGRAPHY

**This academic profile was written by an admissions tutor at Southampton University. The information is useful to all applicants, but some of the advice is pertinent to that department in particular.**

## SUBJECT OVERVIEW

I walk into our control room, with its panoply of views of the sea. There are the updated global pictures from the remote sensors on satellites, there the evolving maps of subsurface variables, there the charts that show the position and status of all our Slocum scientific platforms, and I am

satisfied that we are looking at the ocean more intensely and more deeply than anyone anywhere else. **"**
**HENRY STOMMEL, THE SLOCUM MISSION, 1989**

The above statement summarises the fundamental changes that oceanography has experienced in the last two decades because of the major advances in marine technology. Studying oceanography involves interdisciplinary studies and research in estuarine, coastal and open-ocean environments. Oceanography includes many scientific fields such as physics, geology, chemistry, biology, meteorology, geography, and geodesy. In addition to oceanography, a broad range of course opportunities are available involving different disciplines and technologies from remote sensing to molecular biology.

Because being an oceanographer is about studying the ocean, most oceanographers spend a great deal of time at sea. During the degree, lectures provide the theoretical background to the subject area, laboratory practicals and fieldwork provide hands-on training in experimental activities and surveying techniques. During the degree, students have the opportunity to conduct real-time studies in coastal waters of the UK and abroad using advanced underwater instrumentation. These involve the application of knowledge acquired in biological, chemical, physical and geological processes, deep-sea biology, satellite technology, ocean modelling, fish biology, ocean optics, biodiversity and marine molecular biology.

All students receive training in professional key skills such as scientific writing, oral presentations and poster presentations, which are the key to excelling and succeeding as a professional oceanographer, regardless of the career path the student chooses. Being taught by academics who are active researchers, students acquire first-hand learning about the latest developments of oceanography. In summary, this is an exciting time to be an oceanographer!

## WHAT SKILLS OR ATTRIBUTES DO ADMISSIONS TUTORS LOOK FOR IN A GOOD APPLICANT?

You should display a drive and enthusiasm for – and an informed understanding of – the degree programme(s) for which you have applied. You should be able to demonstrate that you have thoroughly researched the subject area and have considered why you wish to undertake such a degree in the context of your future career development. You will be expected to have ensured that your academic background and the examinations you have yet to take are acceptable, and that your qualifications will be good enough to ensure admission to the course of your choice.

You should provide sufficient information in your Personal Statement to indicate that you not only appreciate the personal skills and abilities required for successful completion of an earth science degree, but that you can illustrate such an appreciation with pertinent personal examples in the form of education-based experiences (for example, personal and team-based sporting or musical activities), extracurricular or work experiences. If you can provide evidence or demonstrate well-developed time and personal management skills, English language, grammar and numerical skills, along with a degree of independence, these are all aspects of your character that will be of interest to admissions staff.

## WHAT DOES A GOOD PERSONAL STATEMENT LOOK LIKE?

Your Personal Statement should convey to an admissions tutor that you not only have a drive and enthusiasm for the degree programme(s) for which you are applying, but also that you have thoroughly researched the subject area and considered why you wish to undertake such a degree in the context of your future career development. As a potential applicant you will be expected to tailor your Personal Statement to address your interest in the wider subject discipline and perhaps in specific areas of the discipline. To realise this you may choose to draw upon your own experiences in AS/A2 level subjects, involvement in subject-related extracurricular activities or work experience. This part of the statement ought to comprise some 30–50% of the whole statement, and should be reflective and demonstrate self-awareness. As all earth and marine science subject areas will have a practical, field-based component, you ought to highlight any such experience and skills which you already have, be it study-based (for example, A levels), or extracurricular (for example, Duke of Edinburgh's Award scheme, Operation Raleigh, or activity-style holidays you have organised for yourself).

However, many of the personal skills and abilities required for successful completion of an earth or marine science degree can also be demonstrated by reference to other forms of education-based experience (for example, personal and individual or team-based sporting or musical activities), or work experience. If you can provide evidence for time and personal management skills and independence, these are all aspects of your character that will be of interest to admissions staff. Avoid meaningless literary quotes or apparent deep thoughtful insights about your chosen topic that you have picked off a website or invented – admissions tutors have read most of them already!

## Example of a good Personal Statement

I have always been fascinated by how the different landscapes in our world have been shaped and formed by the physical workings of the planet. I am particularly interested in oceanography, physical geography and the earth systems, including plate tectonics. My study of the mechanisms of river and coastal processes has inspired me to research physical and human impact on the environment. The current debate around climate change adds a further dimension to my interests. Will the film The Inconvenient Truth influence future decisions regarding energy consumption and America's new involvement in tackling climate change and greenhouse emissions? I look forward to exploring the political and ethical elements involved in the debate with equally enthusiastic tutors and fellow students.

I have enjoyed developing my teamwork skills on field trips to Lulworth Cove and at Slapton. In Slapton, I collected river data along the River Lemon and examined results with computer models using 'live' data from the field, and then I used theoretical skills to analyse and evaluate these results. I hope that my fieldwork at school will have helped me prepare for university.

A level ICT is helping me use various applications to support my research work in A level Geography and Biology. I really enjoy biology as, like geography, it is about the evolution, adaptation and development of organisms. Its appeal is that it complements my work on the physical development of the Earth and the human impact upon it.

Completing the Duke of Edinburgh's Bronze, Silver and Gold Awards was physically and mentally challenging. Attaining grade 4 flute, playing in the school orchestra, and passing my driving test are some of the varied skills I have enjoyed and acquired. While on the Isle of Arran, I really enjoyed the challenge of studying the environment and how it was shaped by geographical and geological processes.

I am a keen gymnast and I really enjoy sports, in particular tennis, hockey and netball. As part of my community service I qualified as an assistant gymnastics coach. I hope that I can use these skills while at university so that I can be part of the university and the local community.

This year I was elected a school prefect. My subject responsibilities are geography and information and communication technology. As part of my role as a geography prefect, I am currently in the process of developing a Geography Society. This will include arranging debates about current geographical issues and organising other activities such as model making and quizzes. I am also involved in helping host a 'World Wide Quiz' for local schools. Other roles include responsibility for junior school and being minute secretary for meetings for the headmistress and prefects. I am also part of a team involved in the development of a new school prospectus. I have improved my organisation and communication skills through involvement in school events and working closely with the parents' committee at social and fundraising events.

I enjoy travelling and last year I went to Russia with an Irish dance school, visiting Moscow and Perm. This trip gave me the chance to see a different culture and landscape as we travelled through the taiga on the Trans-Siberian Express. The isolated rural villages with few resources were especially interesting and memorable.

I look forward to studying geography to degree level. I believe I am positive, enthusiastic and able to manage my academic and extracurricular activities, and feel I am well prepared for the challenge of university life and all that it has to offer.

 ## TOP TIPS

**1** Ensure your qualifications meet published admissions criteria for the particular degree course for which you are applying before you even start to write your Personal Statement!

**2** Provide honest and reflective comments about why you wish to study at university and what you want to achieve in your Personal Statement and pay attention to presentation (for

 ## THINGS TO AVOID

**1** Applying for courses without having checked you have the correct qualifications to offer

**2** Using literary quotes, or unlikely and apparently deeply thoughtful insights about your degree subject to try and impress in your Personal Statement

**3** Applying to courses that you do not feel passionate about. This lack of passion is often evident in the Personal Statement example, checking for correct spelling and grammar)

**4** Being careless with the writing of the application: for example, not checking for spelling mistakes, missing information required by the admissions team. Not being professional is a bad sign for any admissions tutor and any future employer!

##  RECOMMENDED READING AND WEBSITES

- *Discover*: www.discovermagazine.com
- Geologists' Association: www.geologists.org.uk
- *National Geographic*: www.nationalgeographic.com
- *Nature*: www.nature.com
- *New Scientist*: www.newscientist.com
- Royal Geographical Society: www.rgs.org

I am grateful to the oceanography department at Southampton University (www. noc.soton.ac.uk) for their support in writing this profile. Other highly rated courses can be found at the universities of Bangor, UEA, Liverpool and Plymouth.

# PERFORMING ARTS

**This academic profile was written using information provided by an admissions tutor at Liverpool Institute for the Performing Arts (LIPA). The information is useful to all applicants, but some of the advice is pertinent to LIPA in particular.**

## SUBJECT OVERVIEW

A degree course in acting not only provides technical training and the building of a secure acting process but also encourages students to think of their work in a broader context and teaches them to plan, prepare, research and adapt, all of which are important for the actor.

# WHAT SKILLS OR ATTRIBUTES DO ADMISSIONS TUTORS LOOK FOR IN A GOOD APPLICANT?

Academically, most departments are looking for a person with five GCSE passes at a minimum grade of C or above, normally including English and Maths. In terms of level 3 qualifications LIPA does not specify which subjects you need to study – we are looking for people who achieve a minimum of 180 UCAS tariff points, which should ideally be attained in one of the following ways:

- grade B and C at A level or AVCE level. All A level subjects accepted, excluding General Studies
- 'merit, merit, pass' profile at BTEC National Diploma level
- all equivalent UK and overseas qualifications are also accepted, including Welsh Baccalaureate, Scottish Highers, Welsh, European and International Baccalaureate and Irish Leaving Certificate.

We are interested in your talent and ability as an actor so a level of experience in acting, preferably in a variety of contexts, is definitely something we look for. Your interdisciplinary experience is also important, so we look for your potential to train in a second discipline (for example, directing, singing, dancing). You do not have to be a polished performer – demonstrable potential is equally important. We are also interested in your communication skills and in people who can demonstrate that they are enterprising.

In terms of personality traits, we also look for people who are hungry to learn and can self-manage their learning. A good sense of humour and the ability to work collaboratively are useful traits for an actor. An ability to articulate that you can reflect on your practical experience – whether that is verbally or in writing – is important.

# WHAT DOES A GOOD PERSONAL STATEMENT LOOK LIKE?

The most important thing is to communicate a sense of why you think acting is important. The danger is that you write this in a way that comes across as egocentric. While a level of passion should be evident, your statement should support this with examples of relevant experience. An ability to look beyond the most obviously available opportunities (such as the school play) is an additional factor that can help make you stand out. Simply to say that you have always wanted to be an actor or always had a dream to act is not enough. In addition, any experience that suggests engagement with broader social issues can be a positive reinforcement (for example, voluntary work, travel, responsible roles within school or other organisations).

## Example of a good Personal Statement

> 'All the world's a stage,' Shakespeare once said, and for me this statement is truer than any other. Drama and performing is my passion, ever since a young age my sights have been set on performing at the highest level. Through the years, my desire to achieve my goals of becoming an actress in the West End and to join the Royal Shakespeare Company have become stronger and more focused. I believe that my acceptance into this, one of the leading conservatoires in Britain – if not the world – will be the best starting stepping stone into this highly competitive profession.

✓ This opening paragraph in the applicant's Personal Statement illustrates her passion for a career in acting and demonstrates her focus.

> I am a member of several different theatre groups and musical theatre companies, doing around three public performances locally every year, plus musical reviews regularly for local charity events and private functions. My membership to one of these groups, also afforded me the invaluable experience of performing in the National Theatre, London, as part of the Youth Theatre Shell Connections Festival in 2003. Therefore, I feel that my performance experience is definitely a strong point. I have also done professional work for television including extras work in the series Teachers on Channel 4, and in a film to be screened around October 2006 called Outlaw.

✓ This paragraph demonstrates that the applicant has experience in a range of contexts and has an understanding of the differences involved in acting in different contexts. She has been doing reviews for local charity events and private functions, which suggests enterprise. And we can only agree with her statement 'therefore I feel that my performance experience is definitely a strong point'. She has clearly made the effort to get herself involved with a lot of acting activities.

> As well as a great interest in drama/theatre and musicals, I am a keen sportswoman, achieving a place in the Welsh development netball squad in 2004, and I have a strong interest in dance and movement, also attaining a trained level of stage combat and movement. Other interests that I have include art, languages, reading and singing. As a musician, I have also achieved grade 5 singing, grade 5 in flute and in violin grade 3. I also have a keen interest in composing and being a lyricist.

✓ This last paragraph demonstrates that she is trainable in more than one discipline (movement and music). She also engages in other forms of social activity, outside of the performing arts, as she identifies her achievements in netball. Stage combat is also relevant to the acting course. Her interest in art, languages and reading suggest an all round general sense of enquiry about the world.

Another candidate says:

> Being a member of two drama companies for five years gave me the experience to broaden my horizons by attaining a speaking part on Her Benny, which was held in the Liverpool Empire in 2002. After this I acquired a taste for the stage and knew I wanted to perform professionally on the West End. I went on to further my performing experience in the world of film by working for three years as an extra and had small parts with Mersey Television. Also playing a main role in a short film for trainee purposes helped me improve my skills in front of the camera.

✓ This shows a good breadth of acting experience and also enterprise. The applicant is clearly committed because he has sought out these acting opportunities.

> Working part time behind the bar at my local sports and social club and weekends at my local supermarket has improved my communication and social skills, which enables me to interact well with others.

✓ This suggests he is good at managing his time. He must be self-disciplined to manage to fit this work in, on top of his studies. It's also good that he perceived the benefits of improving his communication and social skills.

> I am looking forward to focusing on all aspects of performing arts in more depth, facing new challenges and meeting different people throughout my time at university. I hope to further acquire a variety of skills that will benefit me in life and in my chosen career.

✓ This last paragraph shows his focus and suitability for our course, plus a hunger to learn and recognition about the benefits that come from meeting different people.

The following advice comes in part from a recent LIPA graduate. The advice is good for anyone applying to study acting at any of the major schools.

 **TOP TIPS**

**1** See as much theatre or performance art as possible.

 **THINGS TO AVOID**

**1** Leaving preparation to the last minute: you will not be able to

Watching with an interested and critical eye helps you in so many ways. If you can look at others with a critical eye, you can also look at yourself in the same way. Make sure that you mention your recent experience in your statement

**2** You must be certain that the course you choose to apply for is right for you. Be thorough in your research of the course and institution. You need to do everything you can to be confident in your choices. This confidence in the course should be obvious in your statement: tell the tutor that you have done the right research and know that this is the course for you

**3** Sell your achievements in a positive way: do not undersell yourself and, where you can, mention any performance, production, directing or other relevant experience that you have

learn that Shakespeare speech on the train to LIPA or any other acting school!

**2** Careless errors in your statement

**3** Anything that you cannot defend or discuss at interview

**4** Copying from another source

---

 ## RECOMMENDED READING AND WEBSITES

■ Dee Pilgrim, *Careers Uncovered: Performing Arts*, 2nd edition, Trotman Publishing, 2007

I am grateful to LIPA (www.lipa.ac.uk) for their assistance in writing this profile. Other highly regarded courses can be found at the universities of Middlesex, Roehampton and Edge Hill.

# PHILOSOPHY

This academic profile was written by an admissions tutor at King's College, University of London. The information is useful to all applicants, but some of the advice is pertinent to King's in particular.

## SUBJECT OVERVIEW

Philosophy is one of the oldest and most fundamental academic disciplines that examine the nature of the universe and humanity's place in it. It explores the essence of mind, language, morality and physical reality, and discusses the methods used to investigate these topics. Studying philosophy at university will give you the chance to get to grips with these themes by reading and discussing what great philosophers have had to say about them and forming your own ideas, at the same time developing your powers of logical and creative thinking.

## WHAT SKILLS OR ATTRIBUTES DO ADMISSIONS TUTORS LOOK FOR IN A GOOD APPLICANT?

We are looking for students who enjoy thinking about fundamental questions in a logical way. The ability to express yourself clearly both orally and in writing is important. Students who do well at philosophy tend to be open-minded and able to take and receive criticism freely but fairly. Since philosophy rarely reaches definitive answers to the questions it poses, a sense of curiosity is vital but patience can also be a useful attribute. You do not have to study philosophy formally at school, though we do like to see some evidence of your interest in the subject. Competition for entry is high in many of the best departments. As a result the standard offers are now as high as AAB at King's and similar standard departments.

# WHAT DOES A GOOD PERSONAL STATEMENT LOOK LIKE?

The most important thing is that you write clearly why you want to study philosophy at university and show some evidence of your interest in the subject. Tutors need to see some evidence of this in your reading so far. You do not need to have read all the major works and even be particularly expert in any. However, they would hope to see evidence that you have read one of the better general introductions to the subject and one of the more accessible philosophers' works. Plato's *Republic* is a good introductory text, as is Mill's *Utilitarianism*. Tutors hope to read a statement that is clear, concise and precise in its presentation. Philosophy is, after all, a subject that is essentially transmitted orally and on paper. If you are applying for a joint honours degree, that is fine, as long as both subjects are included in your statement.

Tutors are predominantly interested in your academic profile but also keen to hear about your extracurricular pursuits.

 ## TOP TIPS

**1** Talk about why you are interested in studying philosophy. This should be an obvious point, but a significant number of applicants, particularly those applying for joint degrees, say nothing or very little about why they want to do philosophy

**2** Mention a few books on philosophy that you have read, and what you found of value in them. Do not just give a reading list

**3** If you are also applying for other subjects, feel free to say so, but don't neglect the first two tips!

**4** Break your statement up into sections (not too many);

 ## THINGS TO AVOID

**1** Supplying lots of unnecessary detail about your hobbies and travel abroad – although foreign travel might be more relevant to applications for other subjects, especially modern languages

**2** Writing at length about how wonderful you think philosophy is and/or how passionate you are about it – tutors like to see enthusiasm, but be concise and specific rather than vague and general

**3** Using jargon and technical vocabulary that you don't understand, just because it sounds impressive – it may don't write it as one continuous paragraph

**5** Write clearly and grammatically, and avoid spelling errors

**6** Make sure that you proofread your statement properly and that it flows well

impress your friends (though it may not), but it won't fool an experienced university teacher

**4** Explaining at length why you want to do a degree other than the one for which you have applied, or at another institution

**5** Boasting: let your achievements speak for themselves

**6** Plagiarising your personal statement: a serious error of judgement!

 ## RECOMMENDED READING AND WEBSITES

- Nigel Warburton, *Philosophy: The Basics*, Routledge, 2004
- Simon Blackburn, *Think: A Compelling Introduction to Philosophy*, Oxford Paperbacks, 2001
- Plato, *The Republic*

I am grateful to the philosophy department at King's College, London (www.kcl. ac.uk/schools/humanities/depts/philosophy) for their support in compiling this profile. Other highly rated courses can be found at the universities of Oxford, Cambridge, St Andrew's, LSE and Stirling.

# PHYSICS

This academic profile was written by an admissions tutor at Bath University and focuses on physics as a single honours discipline. The information is useful to all applicants, but please be aware that some of the advice is pertinent to that department in particular.

## SUBJECT OVERVIEW

Physics is the fundamental science; it is concerned with the study of matter, energy and the interactions between them, and it involves the search for the universal principles underlying many, very diverse natural phenomena. It is important not only as a subject in its own right, but also as an essential element in all other natural sciences, engineering and technology. There is also a great deal of enjoyment and satisfaction to be derived from an understanding of the most recent developments in physics research.

Physics graduates combine sound mathematical and experimental expertise with the ability to grasp new concepts and are able to apply their expertise to many familiar and unfamiliar challenges. Physics often involves the development of mathematical models of complex behaviour and develops the judgment and imagination necessary to solve problems at an appropriate level of approximation. The development of many other important skills – such as written and verbal communication, computational skills, and teamworking – is embedded in physics degree programmes.

The versatility of physics is reflected in the wide variety of occupations in which they may be found. Nearly all modern industries call on the insight and technical expertise of physicists. Physicists are equally valued for the contribution they can make to education, administration, business and commerce, where their problem-solving skills are in great demand.

## WHAT SKILLS OR ATTRIBUTES DO ADMISSIONS TUTORS LOOK FOR IN A GOOD APPLICANT?

The most important attributes are a high level of competence in mathematics and physics, with particular emphasis on the former, and an enthusiasm for the study of physics. Admissions tutors also look for good communication skills, and evidence of ability to work alone or in groups. However, most students exhibit a tremendous diversity of personalities and interests, and we are very pleased that this is the case: anoraks are not required!

# WHAT DOES A GOOD PERSONAL STATEMENT LOOK LIKE?

Your statement is going to be read by five admissions tutors from five different departments – so avoid being too specific in stating your interests – for example, not every department offers cosmology options; do not betray your first choice(s); do not say that you have always wanted to be a mathematician if you are applying for both mathematics and physics programmes, or even for joint degree programmes; if you are applying to physics programmes as an alternative to a medical degree, then make this clear in your statement (for example, do not just mention medicine).

We look for good grammatical construction and good motivation. Be original – don't just write what you think you should, and definitely don't download – without being quirky for the sake of it. Anything you write about is fair game if you are interviewed, when you will be expected to be able to talk about anything in your statement – so be honest.

## Example of a good Personal Statement

At Bath, in common with most other physics departments in the country, we pay most attention to academic achievement and potential as contained primarily in A level grades (or equivalent). We rarely reject a student because of a Personal Statement; in our experience, most statements are written adequately. Any statement written following the guidelines above would be acceptable. However, in the case of a student who has narrowly missed their offer grades, we may look to your statement for signs of something special.

Students generally begin by expressing their interest in and commitment to physics as a discipline, provide some evidence of this – usually in the form of reading matter and short events they have attended – and end with a description of their other activities and interests. Such statements are fine, but generally contain nothing to catch the eye. The following example is good because it is brief, honest and to the point:

> I have chosen to study physics at university as I want to study a subject that is not only universally useful but is always crossing new frontiers of knowledge.

✓ A good start, and not too flowery.

> Physics has always interested me. . .

✗ Cliché alert!

> . . .and I particularly want to continue with it as studying the subject over the years has brought just as many new questions to me as it has answered. I have always tried to keep up to date with scientific developments and as such I read issues of New Scientist and I have currently been reading the Richard Feynman lectures.

✓ This is good because it avoids reference to Stephen Hawking!

> In July 2006, I attended a three-day physics course at XYZ University.

✓ Excellent.

> This was a valuable experience, involving problem solving exercises and sample lectures, which gave me an insight into the areas of physics in which I would be most interested in specialising. Nanoscience is an area that consequently attracted me due to its interdisciplinary nature, as it can be applied to practically everything, from electronics to engineering, to biology and the environment. I'm sure there will be great progress in this field in the near future.
>    I have applied for MPhys/MSci courses as I am keen to pursue a career in research, and as such my shortlist of universities have all been selected for their strong research facilities.

✓ Shows that some research has been done into which choices to make.

> Aside from Mathematics and Physics, I also chose my A levels to cater for analytical skills and to keep up a well-rounded education. Classics was a completely new subject to me and I was interested in taking on something fresh. History provided more breadth to my A levels, and I think it is important to be well informed, particularly on aspects of modern world history. Both of these subjects have the bonus of maintaining my fluency in essay writing.
>    I enjoy music and I am an avid guitarist. I play acoustic, bass and particularly electric to a very high standard. I frequently play with others for entertainment and have posted videos of performance on the internet which received very pleasing feedback. I also write music, and aside from my own compositions I am working on a number of joint projects with a friend. My experience of playing the guitar had even come in useful in studying the waves part of the A2 Physics syllabus last year, as I found that I had encountered many phenomena such as resonance and standing waves, and had in fact taken advantage of these for musical effect.

✓ Evidence of interests outside school.

> In researching courses, I was encouraged to see the large investment currently being made in physics departments, and I am certain there are many interesting developments in which I can become involved.

✓ Shows evidence of research into his chosen universities.

## Examples from poor Personal Statements

The next examples are taken from the beginnings of statements representing the vast majority we receive, which are unlikely to catch the eye.

> Ever since an early age I have been fascinated by physics, in particular how and why things work and how vast the subject of physics is. . .

> Ever since school I have been interested in sciences. . .

> Physics has always intrigued me. . .

> My interest in physics was first awakened when I read A Brief History of Time by Stephen Hawking at the age of 13. . .

> The wonders of earth and space have interested me from an early age. . .

> For many years I have been interested in the sciences. . .

> I was fascinated by science and maths from my first years at secondary school. . .

> From an early age I have wanted to study physics so that I can attempt to understand the universe around me. . .

> When I was a child I always asked, why? I'm now 18 and I still do.

✗ Two examples of misdirected statements (applications to read single-subject physics):

> I hold a strong desire to study Physics and Philosophy at university.

Since a very young age, I have had a strong desire to become a doctor.

## TOP TIPS

**1** Find out as much about the course as you can so that you can talk about specific elements that interest you, and why, in your Personal Statement

**2** Make sure you have good reasons for applying to your chosen courses and explain these in your statement

**3** Try and be original with your opening statement without being quirky. Admissions tutors have to read hundreds of statements so something more unusual is more likely to catch their interest

**4** Refer to your A level (or equivalent) courses and demonstrate how these will prepare you for degree level study of physics

**5** Give evidence of other interests and show how these have given you additional skills that will be useful for university level study

## THINGS TO AVOID

**1** A poorly constructed statement, full of grammatical errors and clichés

**2** Writing fanciful prose, especially in the opening sentence

**3** Mentioning specialities not relevant to some of your chosen departments

**4** Mentioning your top choice(s) – you may change your mind!

**5** Saying you have read Stephen Hawking's *A Brief History of Time*. You may well have done this (at least partly!), and this is commendable, but we read this statement in a large fraction of our applications and it has become a kind of cliché which does not lift you above the crowd

## RECOMMENDED READING AND WEBSITES

- Institute of Physics: www.iop.org
- Nexus: www.iop.org/activity/nexus. Student wing of the Institute of Physics

I am grateful to the University of Bath (www.bath.ac.uk) for their support in compiling this profile. Other highly rated courses can be found at the universities of Oxford, Birmingham, UCL, Imperial and Leeds.

# PHYSIOTHERAPY

**This academic profile was written by an admissions tutor at Brighton University. The information in this profile is useful to all applicants, but some of the advice is pertinent to Brighton in particular.**

## SUBJECT OVERVIEW

Physiotherapy is an absorbing and fascinating way of working with people in a positive way to improve or maintain their health. Physiotherapists work with people mainly through the use of exercise and manual therapies to enhance health. Degree programmes in physiotherapy provide both university experience and the experience of working with people in healthcare settings. The students go into clinical settings to work with qualified physiotherapists and other health professionals; for example, nurses, doctors, and occupational therapists. This balance of academic and work-based learning is excellent preparation for a career in healthcare.

If you think you would enjoy working with people in a health setting there is plenty of scope for you to develop many technical, academic and interpersonal skills. All physiotherapy degrees need to carry eligibility for state registration, enabling graduates to practise as physiotherapists and be approved by the professional body – the Chartered Society of Physiotherapists.

## WHAT SKILLS OR ATTRIBUTES DO ADMISSIONS TUTORS LOOK FOR IN A GOOD APPLICANT?

We are looking for enthusiastic people who have a good academic profile from a wide range of educational experiences and who are prepared to learn. We would like to recruit students who are motivated and have made the effort to find out about physiotherapy. We are particularly keen on people who have had the opportunity to observe different aspects of physiotherapy and are able to explain why they are interested in developing a career in the area.

Most good departments will expect a candidate to have at least one science A level (or equivalent) – preferably Biology or Chemistry. Where two sciences are not offered at A2, another is often required at AS.

Entry standards vary, but most departments now make offers of BBB rising to ABB (or their equivalent). The course consists of theory and practice – a large part of the emphasis at the University of Brighton is the acquisition of physiotherapy skills before going on to clinical placements. This would probably be true of other departments in the UK. The styles of teaching are tutorials, practicals, seminars, workshops and lectures – according to what most suits the learning material.

## WHAT DOES A GOOD PERSONAL STATEMENT LOOK LIKE?

It is really helpful, if you have observed some physiotherapy sessions, to briefly describe your experience and explain why you would like to study it. You really need to describe something more varied than a personal experience of receiving physiotherapy – which shows that you have made an effort to see different aspects of physiotherapy – or at least have plans to broaden your understanding. Many departments do not look favourably at an overemphasis on sport. Most physiotherapists work in hospital settings and do not get involved in any form of sports-related injury or rehabilitation.

It is always good to hear about your activities beyond the academic, particularly if you are interested in continuing them at university. If you can, try and show a range of interests other than sport. We are interested in music, drama and other extracurricular pursuits, especially if they show evidence of individual leadership or teamwork skills. If you have had a job or done voluntary work make sure you explain something positive about the experience of interacting with people.

Try and find a balance between self-promotion, explaining your recent experiences of work, social activities and school achievements. Overemphasis on any of these elements can skew your statement.

## Example of a good Personal Statement

> I have shadowed a sports physiotherapist and spent time in an NHS hospital, where I shadowed both junior and senior physiotherapists in all wards; this, combined with my own personal research of the career by means of literature and talking with many physiotherapists, has served to increase my desire to commit myself to a career as a physiotherapist.

✓ Shows that an effort has been made beyond personal experience and that active research has been made to understand physiotherapy.

> The diversity in the roles astounded me, ranging from the intricacies of the hand clinic to the very manual rehabilitation of stroke patients, where constant feed back on posture and walking gait is given. Despite the various techniques employed, several competencies became very evident to me: a physiotherapist is an excellent communicator, problem solving team player who can work holistically with other members of a multidisciplinary team whose goals are to educate and rehabilitate a patient so that they may return to everyday life as speedily as possible.

✓ Shows some well-informed opinion.

> Having travelled and met people from many different backgrounds and age groups, I am confident that I now possess the maturity and keenness of mind to undertake a physiotherapy degree and meet with enthusiasm any of the challenges that a career as a chartered physiotherapist poses.

✓ A very literate statement, but could also include more personal information about hobbies.

 **TOP TIPS**

**1** Indicate early on your passion for the subject with examples to support this interest

**2** Show that you are interested in current health issues

 **THINGS TO AVOID**

**1** Telling us how much you want to be a nurse/be a doctor/work in the leisure industry!

**2** Writing about anything you are not prepared to talk about at interview

**3** Tell the tutor about your work experience and contact with physiotherapists. Say what you learnt from this experience and how it helped you to make up your mind to apply

**4** Make sure that your science skills are clearly developed in your statement

**5** Write a list of things you have done: be specific and pick out the best

**6** It is always good to hear about your activities beyond the academic, particularly if you are interested in continuing them at university

**7** Try and find a balance between self-promotion, explaining your recent experiences of work, social activities and school achievements. Overemphasis on any of these elements can skew your statement

**3** Writing about sport to the exclusion of all else – many departments do not look favourably at an overemphasis on sport. Most physiotherapists work in hospital settings and do not get involved in any form of sports-related injury or rehabilitation

**4** Confusing physiotherapy and psychotherapy!

**5** Poor spelling, punctuation and grammar – get your statement proofread by a competent teacher or tutor

# RECOMMENDED READING AND WEBSITES

- James Barton, *Getting into Physiotherapy Courses*, 5th edition, Trotman Publishing, 2010

- Reading any current affairs information about health issues and physiotherapy would be good but there are no particular activities other than your natural keenness to pursue a career in physiotherapy. It would make sense to read a book about what it is like to be a physiotherapist; there are a variety on the market that bring the subject to life. The Chartered Society of Physiotherapists has a good website (www.csp.org.uk) with a range of information that would extend your knowledge of the subject

I am grateful to Brighton University (www.brighton.ac.uk) for their support in preparing this profile. Other highly rated courses can be found at the universities of Birmingham, King's College London, Bristol UWE, Southampton and St George's Hospital, London.

# PODIATRY

**This academic profile was written by an admissions tutor at Brighton University. The information is useful to all applicants, but some of the advice is pertinent to Brighton in particular.**

## SUBJECT OVERVIEW

Chiropodists (now often called podiatrists) diagnose and treat abnormalities of the lower limb. They give professional advice on the prevention of foot problems and on proper care of the foot. Patients will be of all ages from infants to the elderly. Working as a podiatrist can be exciting and rewarding because it involves working in a variety of environments with a number of other healthcare professionals and many different groups of patients who have a wide range of podiatric problems.

The scope of practice of a podiatrist is often much wider than many people realise. Some examples of patients are:

- children who sometimes have pains in their legs or feet as they grow or have problems walking
- people with diabetes who may have problems with their circulation or sensation in their feet
- sportsmen and sportswomen, who often suffer from injuries to their legs and feet
- dancers with long hours rehearsing and performing, who put stress through their feet that can cause injury
- people needing minor surgery: some nail surgery or laser treatment
- people wanting advice: some people do not need treatment but just want advice about footwear or foot health.

To become a practitioner registered by the Health Professional Council, there is a requirement to undertake and pass a three-year full-time honours degree in podiatry. The degree also provides eligibility to apply for membership of the Society of Chiropodists and Podiatrists (www.feetforlife.org).

The course at Brighton (along with others in the UK) includes a minimum of four further weeks of external clinical placement with NHS trusts. Students benefit from the multidisciplinary medical team, specialist hospital ward rounds, outpatient clinics and orthopaedic operating sessions. Short placements are arranged with specialist podiatrists and a variety of allied health professionals so that the student experiences as wide a range of podiatric care as possible.

The podiatry undergraduate programme is very intensive and requires considerable dedication on the part of the student.

## WHAT SKILLS OR ATTRIBUTES DO ADMISSIONS TUTORS LOOK FOR IN A GOOD APPLICANT?

The normal minimum entrance requirements are GCSE C or above in English, Mathematics and Science with an additional expectation that the student will, on average, obtain 240 tariff points or above at AS or A2 or equivalent, usually including a science subject. Mature students enter the programme by a variety of routes, the most common being approved standard Access courses. Entrance requirements may differ for courses at other universities.

You should be well motivated to learn and have an enthusiasm to study at degree level. You should also be fully committed to this area of work.

Communication is probably the most important skill a healthcare worker should possess. You should be able to communicate effectively both verbally and in writing. Although you will be helped to develop these skills during the course of your degree, having well developed interpersonal skills will help you in both the practice learning and theoretical aspects of this programme.

The administration of local anaesthesia and the appreciation of mechanics and statistics in podiatry mean that an understanding of mathematics is required to this level. Computer technology is used extensively in healthcare and it is therefore important that your ICT skills are developed. Basic word processing, spreadsheet and internet search skills are therefore essential on enrolment, while you can develop others such as PowerPoint during the programme.

## WHAT DOES A GOOD PERSONAL STATEMENT LOOK LIKE?

**Motivation and commitment:** podiatry is a fascinating subject and a stimulating profession and practitioners are privileged to have working relationships with some of the most vulnerable members of our society. You should show an appreciation of the scope of podiatry and the role of the podiatrist within the multidisciplinary healthcare team, and should be able to indicate that you are fully committed to this area of work.

**Interpersonal skills:** as communication is probably the most important skill a healthcare worker should possess, you will need to consider how you have demonstrated effective communication in your life. This would ideally be communication to a mixed audience, using a variety of methods, and perhaps even at different levels.

**Interest in working and learning as part of a team:** admissions tutors will be looking for skills of working with others towards a shared goal and operating as part of a team. After-school activities such as debating societies and membership of sports teams can be used as examples of this. Other evidence can be drawn from appropriate discussion of previous life experiences.

**Dexterity:** practical podiatry requires a high level of dexterity. Applications should include their acquisition of these skills, for example the practice of art and craft skills, the playing of a musical instrument, the skills of design and technology.

## Example from a good Personal Statement

The following applicant demonstrated all the qualities our admissions team look for, both by the written word and by using specific examples. Her statement was logical in presentation, well written and with a wide vocabulary, and gave consideration to the attributes a healthcare worker should possess.

> I have always been captivated by the human body and how it can perform the most complex of tasks without conscious thought. Because of this fascination, I chose to study Human Biology and Psychology at A2 level, as well as Sports Studies at AS. Through these subjects I have been able to learn more about the mechanics of the body and the relationship of body and mind.

✓ She has attempted to link both the human physiology with the working of the brain, demonstrating an appreciation that podiatry is about psychosocial issues, not just biology.

> I am also studying AVCE Health and Social Care (6 units). [She could have perhaps made more of this here, but the remainder of her statement illustrates why this was an important statement.] Having always aspired to a career in healthcare, I have decided to pursue a degree in podiatry. Having researched the subject thoroughly, I find the scope of opportunities within the profession very exciting.

✓ Shows she has actively looked for information, particularly career choices.

> Biomechanics is an area that fascinates me. Having enjoyed the academic study of anatomy and physiology in my A levels, I am eager to combine this theory with practical applications.

✓ Shows an appreciation that textbook biology needs translating into applied practice.

> I am also keen to learn more about the surgical aspect of podiatry. As part of my Health and Social Care course I have had the opportunity to take part in a weekly work experience placement at a podiatry clinic. Through this I have been able to gain an invaluable insight into the profession in a clinical environment. I am learning first-hand about the practical and theoretical side of podiatry, which has further confirmed my desire to study this subject.

✓ This demonstrates motivation and commitment, and that she had been exposed to a reasonable scope of practice of a podiatrist.

> Outside school I have worked in retail. From this I have gained experience in the real world, undertaking responsibilities and learning to work with a wide range of people. I enjoy meeting and talking with customers, establishing their needs and having the satisfaction of being able to help them. I have won two awards for my customer service skills.

✓ Communication skills are evidenced here, along with the appreciation that healthcare offers a service to a wide audience. She also illustrates her sense of responsibility.

> Working with other employees in a team has hugely improved my communication skills, but I also enjoy the challenges of using my own initiative. This has greatly improved my self-confidence.

✓ Podiatrists work as part of a team, but for much of their practice they have to work in single chair clinics. This applicant is demonstrating an understanding of the importance of both modes of working.

> My interest in human biology drove me to learn first aid. I am now a fully trained volunteer first aider and cadet leader with St John Ambulance. I devote most of my spare time to organising cadet activities and providing first aid cover at local events.

✓ Here she is showing evidence not only for her skills in caring but her ability to deal with accidents and events that could involve blood and other traumatic situations. She is also communicating that she has a sense of moral obligation and a strong work ethic, that she can cope with stress, has energy and can organise herself and other people.

> Due to the nature of the work I have to communicate effectively and sensitively with a cross-section of people, often in highly stressful situations. I love the work I do and get a great a satisfaction from being involved in something so rewarding. I can play the piano and have recently taken my grade 8. In my spare time I like to listen to music and read novels. Jane Eyre is a particular favourite of mine.

✓ Dexterity skills are shown here, along with a rounded approach to life.

> From the experiences I have gained I believe that podiatry is not only the subject I will thoroughly enjoying studying, but that it will provide me with a rewarding long-term career.

 **TOP TIPS**

**1** Your enthusiasm for the subject should be clear in the opening paragraph. Think about ways in which this enthusiasm can be transmitted. If at all possible, arrange to meet a practising podiatrist and include what you learnt from this meeting in your statement – this will give you a real edge

 **THINGS TO AVOID**

**1** Not being sure what podiatry is: before you apply make sure that you read up about the subject – indicate this level of research in your statement

**2** Mumbling at interview

**3** Failing to support or develop points made in your statement at interview

**2** The tutors expect to see a well-written statement that shows off your ability to communicate well. Elsewhere they need to see evidence of your ability to work in teams and communicate effectively to others orally

**3** An engaging personality should come across in your statement and later at interview

**4** Manual dexterity is a vital part of the assessment process, any evidence you can provide of an ability to use your hands to make, repair or design will be welcome

**5** Show that you have a rounded approach to life, including studies: tell tutors about your interests, particularly those that include a need for independence, initiative and teamwork

**4** Poor spelling, punctuation and grammar

**5** A statement that is uninspiring, lacking in detail about your skills and desire to study this particular vocation

## RECOMMENDED READING AND WEBSITES

■ Chartered Society of Podiatrists: www.feetforlife.org

I am grateful to the University of Brighton for their assistance in compiling this profile. Other highly rated courses can be found at the universities of Glasgow Caledonian, Plymouth, Southampton and Ulster.

# PSYCHOLOGY

## SUBJECT OVERVIEW

A degree in psychology, as well as being extremely interesting, provides a very wide range of employment prospects to its graduates. Modern psychology is a genuine science in its infancy, trying to understand one of the most fascinating systems ever – the human mind. It is a little like studying physics in the days when gravity was just being understood; the field is changing all the time and is rich with new questions to be answered.

Many students (including those who have taken the subject at A level) are surprised about how much of a modern psychology degree concerns experiments testing rigorous hypotheses and studies of brain processes, but they usually learn to appreciate the need for solid data-based theories.

# WHAT SKILLS OR ATTRIBUTES DO ADMISSIONS TUTORS LOOK FOR IN A GOOD APPLICANT?

As a multidisciplinary subject, few subject-specific skills are required to make a good candidate, other than logical reasoning and the ability to learn. Some of our students come from pure arts backgrounds and really excel at the essay writing; some come from pure science and are very strong in the experimental and analytical components; and some have multidisciplinary backgrounds. We find that any combination can work very well. We do normally expect candidates' subjects to be broadly academic – psychology is no soft option at university level and we do want to know that students have developed some of the above skills during their sixth-form period.

In terms of personality, the best students are usually just dedicated and keen. Students who can focus their minds on the task at hand and push themselves will do well. Often that comes down to the fact that they find the subject interesting and are more willing to work hard at it. Psychology students are often outgoing and dynamic but these personal attributes are certainly not necessary for successful selection.

University life is very different from school. There is a much bigger drive to encourage 'autonomous learning' in students, fostering the ability to explore topics themselves. Formal teaching is often in much larger groups – lectures may have several hundred students – and is aimed more at providing the initial basis for the students' learning rather than providing the entire syllabus. Some universities still talk about 'reading for a degree', reflecting the greater amount of time spent in libraries than classes.

## WHAT DOES A GOOD PERSONAL STATEMENT LOOK LIKE?

Think about your target audience – the admissions tutor. That person's job is to try and work out whether or not you will perform well on their course.

You need to show that a) you know a little about the subject and b) you really want to study it. These are good indicators of your dedication to the course because if you enjoy the material you are keener to work on it. You might show this in different ways; you might want to explain why you are interested in the course if there is some compelling reason that you have always been fascinated by the discipline. You might be able to use evidence of additional work or reading that you have carried out in the topic or demonstrate your knowledge of the subject. Obviously, either of these routes should refer to real aspects of contemporary psychology. Reading a psychology journal will stand you in better stead than owning the box set of *Cracker*.

One problem for the admissions tutor is trying to work out how generous you are being with the truth. According to most Personal Statements and references, all students are confident, independent, sociable, intellectual types with excellent debating skills. In reality some students are terrified, some are not very keen to question and some are at university because they didn't want to get a job yet. The difficulty can be in working out which students are which. You can help here by showing your skills rather than explaining them. Some students will tell us that they subscribe to *Psychological Bulletin*, but others will discuss a psychological issue that they find interesting. By discussing the issue accurately they demonstrate their interest in a way that is harder to fake, which saves the admissions tutor worrying whether it is a lie.

Extracurricular activities may help to show your ability to achieve your goals and your ability to manage your time (if combined with good grades) but do not go overboard. In particular, do not spend a great deal of time describing pastimes that are not likely to make you a better student. Ultimately an admissions tutor will be more interested in how well you get through the course than your love of film or your social charisma. We also want to see a wide variety of personalities. Imagine a department where everyone was gregarious and confident – it would be painful!

Also bear in mind that the way you write your statement is going to be direct evidence for the admissions tutor of how well you write. Make sure your statement is clear, expressive and accurate. Read through it several times and get someone else to read it. If your Personal Statement is littered with errors, an admissions tutor will not believe the reference when it discusses your excellent essay-writing skills.

Your Personal Statement is also a time to discuss anything unusual about your qualifications so far. An admissions tutor might be interested in students whose grades haven't previously been as good as they should if they have a convincing explanation that this will change. Some students thrive at university while others suffer from the independent style of learning. Dedication to the course goes a long way. Also, students who have chosen unusual, or less academic, subjects can use this space to explain what the subject is or how it has been beneficial to them in preparing for a psychology degree. Bear in mind that a university lecturer might not realise how much essay writing you had to do, or how much maths is involved in your particular course. The basic skills you develop in your sixth form are at least as useful as the specific knowledge you have, so English and maths are likely to be at least as useful subjects to take as psychology itself.

## Example from a good Personal Statement

The following student was taking History, Music and Biology A levels as well as General Studies and an AS level in French. Although she has never studied psychology formally, she demonstrates her enthusiasm for the subject throughout her Personal Statement and shows a great deal of energy in both her work and extracurricular pursuits. The statement is written clearly and carefully with appropriate and error-free language. We can have little doubt that the candidate possesses the necessary academic skills, as well as work ethic, to progress very well at university.

Psychology strikes me as the most fascinating area of study imaginable. I love the fact that it is such a diverse subject, ranging from animal behaviour or inter-group relations to child psychology and research methodology. I am particularly intrigued by developmental psychology, especially abnormal psychology in children, and I am keen to learn more about the ways in which an application of this subject can benefit children with conditions such as autism.

✓ This shows understanding of what a diverse range of subjects modern psychology covers.

Through my work as a volunteer with special needs children on summer schemes I have begun to understand more about how autistic children discover and learn, and also how a response to their need for solitude, repetition and a strict routine can often bring them great comfort. I have started to learn sign language and other forms of non-verbal communication, such as PECS, to use in stressful situations where speech may be ineffective. In addition, this work has enabled me to develop my ability to take responsibility, often in demanding situations, and to adapt quickly to difficult circumstances, such as relating to a child whose only form of communication is through spitting. I also enjoyed taking sole care of severely disabled children both in hydrotherapy pools and a sensory room.

I have read a number of books including The Man Who Mistook his Wife for a Hat (Oliver Sachs) and have found Abnormal Psychology (Davison and Neal) useful for reference. I particularly like Margaret Donaldson's Children's Minds as I found Donaldson's criticism of Piaget's theories interesting. Through researching different developmental disorders I was able to gain a better understanding of the individual needs of the children with whom I worked.

✓ She has read around the subject despite not taking any formal course in it and demonstrates that she has read it by discussing the material.

This both enhanced my ability to interact successfully with the children and fuelled my desire to learn and research more on this topic.

I enjoyed reading about current issues in psychology, for example the latest ideas on the 'nature versus nurture' debate. This is reflected in my A level choices of Biology which I feel represents the neurological reasons for actions, and History, which shows how past experiences influence decisions and behaviours.

✓ Explaining your choices of A level subjects is good. Actually, this candidate might have been better to emphasise the skills developed during these courses (in history she will have developed her written fluency) rather than pointing out specific information that has been learned (that behaviour is shaped by previous experience). The skills will be more useful and take much longer to develop.

Music is a passion of mine; I love the teamwork involved in playing in a group as well as the challenge and discipline involved in mastering new pieces. I recently gained grade 8 clarinet with distinction and I also play both violin and piano. I am a member of many different orchestras and ensembles. In the main college orchestra I was leader of the second violins and now lead the clarinet section, and these roles have enabled me to develop and improve my leadership skills. I was one of 16 students in the county awarded a place on the Hampshire Specialist Music Course, which has enhanced my ability to manage my time effectively between music practice and academic work.

In my spare time I have organised and led meetings in my school's theological society and evenings for teenagers at my local youth group, and I have worked full days as a childminder for up to four children at a time. This has helped me to appreciate the endurance and creativity needed to stimulate children in an appropriate way for prolonged periods.

✓ You will be very busy at university. Show, if you can, that you have energy and good time management.

 **TOP TIPS**

**1** Show that you know a little about the subject and that you really want to study it. These are good indicators of your dedication to the course because if you enjoy the material you are keener to work on the more difficult aspects of it

**2** Look at exactly what is taught in the department you are applying to and make sure that you indicate somewhere in your statement that you have done this important research

**3** Check your form and statement for errors carefully: get your statement proofread by someone you trust

**4** Show your skills rather than explain them. Some students will tell us that they subscribe to *Psychological Bulletin*, but others will discuss a psychological issue

 **THINGS TO AVOID**

**1** Discussing, at length, extracurricular activities that do not make you a better student: universities want to take rounded students but stick to the activities that add value to your application in your statement – don't just list them!

**2** Claiming to be widely read on the subject if you actually know little about it: this is often clear when reading the statement and will become clearer if you are called for interview

**3** Forgetting for whom you are writing your statement: an admissions tutor (generally a lecturer in the department)

**4** Using slang, text-speak or off-the-wall humour

that they find interesting. By discussing the issue accurately they demonstrate their interest in a way that is harder to fake, which saves the admissions tutor worrying if it is a lie

---

## RECOMMENDED READING AND WEBSITES

- Owen Davies, *Careers Uncovered: Psychology*, Trotman Publishing, 2009
- Maya Waterstone, *Getting Into Psychology Courses*, 8th edition, Trotman Publishing, 2010

I am grateful for the support I received from the Psychology department at Nottingham (www.nottingham.ac.uk) in the preparation of this profile. Other highly rated courses include those at the universities of Oxford, UCL, St Andrew's, Royal Holloway and Bristol.

# SPORTS AND EXERCISE SCIENCE

**This profile was written using information provided by an admissions tutor for sport and exercise science at the University of Essex but much of the advice here is also relevant to other degree courses involving sport such as sports studies, sports development, sport therapy, and coaching science. Please be aware that some of what follows may be particular to Essex.**

## SUBJECT OVERVIEW

Sports and exercise science is a multidisciplinary subject that covers the physiology, biomechanics and psychology of sport, exercise and physical activity. Students learn how the body responds and adapts to exercise, how and why different energy systems are deployed at different exercise intensities, how the principles of mechanics determine the movement of athletes and objects, how exercise reduces the risk of ill health and how mind and body interact to influence performance. In short, studying sports and exercise science gives students a new perspective on the world of sport, exercise, health and physical fitness.

# WHAT SKILLS OR ATTRIBUTES DO ADMISSIONS TUTORS LOOK FOR IN A GOOD APPLICANT?

Desirable academic skills include good oral and written communication, team work, and some evidence of practical scientific skill. Students on sport-related courses generally have a great personal interest in sport and exercise and tend to participate in sport-related activities in their personal lives. However, excellence in sport is not necessary.

The A level requirements vary between institutions. Admissions tutors will often expect at least one science A2 level (or equivalent) with preference given to biology or physical education. Other good subjects include maths, chemistry or psychology.

# WHAT DOES A GOOD PERSONAL STATEMENT LOOK LIKE?

Demonstrate your knowledge and enthusiasm, both for sports science as an academic discipline and for sport in general. You may want to research the courses you are applying for as sport-related courses can vary in content across institutions. Focus on a couple of aspects which all your chosen courses have in common – such as anatomy or sports psychology. You may want to mention anything you are currently studying which has inspired you to pursue sports science at a higher level. It is certainly a good idea to talk about your extracurricular activities relating to sport and any positions of responsibility these have led to. Highlight if you are keen to continue your involvement when you are at university. However, it is important to focus on your interest in the degree, and why it is your chosen course.

## Examples from a good Personal Statement

> I have chosen to apply for a course involving sport and exercise science because I have always had a genuine love of anything sporting and this is shown by me representing my school in a range of sporting activities. As well as this, I am fascinated by the workings of the body and how exercise affects it.

✓ This opening line immediately shows an interest of all aspects of sport, and demonstrates clear enthusiasm for the subject which is crucial.

> I am taking A levels in Physical Education, Psychology, and Mathematics and am enjoying all my subjects, especially PE. I love physical activity, being taught about how the human body works and applying this to sport. I have also enjoyed studying psychology and mathematics as I can link them with physical education in modules such as sport psychology and biomechanics.

✓ An effective way of linking A level subjects to an overall interest in sports science.

> Recently I completed the 'Step into Sport' volunteering scheme and am awaiting my Gold Award, as I have managed to achieve well over the 200 hours needed for this certificate. Volunteering within sport has presented me with numerous opportunities to develop my personal skills. For example, I coach our school's U13 girls' cricket team, and my leadership and coaching skills helped them to win the indoor and outdoor competition this year; they are currently the best U13 girls' cricket team in the county.

✓ Clear evidence of the student's interest in sport on a practical level. Evidence of coaching experience is also a strong point.

> On Tuesday nights I coach kayaking for people aged between 8 and adult. Coaching kayaking and being a Cub leader has encouraged me to consider becoming a teacher; I love seeing a positive change in children's knowledge and skills.

✓ Mentioning future career aspirations and how you chose them can be effective in a Personal Statement.

> I hope to make use of any further opportunity that arises during my time at university to continue to expand my sporting interests and to make use of my leadership skills in a variety of new situations. I want to get as much out of university as possible and relish the prospect of commencing the next step of my study in a subject that I truly enjoy.

✓ Good summarising final statement, again clearly showing enthusiasm and that the applicant is looking forward to university level study in sports science.

## Examples from a poor Personal Statement

> Through the course of my life there have been many ambitions, attractions and pursuits that have come and gone, for example pastimes in gaming and drawing, a proposed career in photography and girlfriends, but the one thing that has always sustained in terms of longevity throughout my life is my fixation with sports.

✗ This opening line takes a while to get to the point and gives information which is irrelevant. The English is poor; always get it checked.

> The main reason for me selecting this course is my absolute passion and dedication for sport. This is the fundamental point of this statement and my application to your university.

✗ This sentence is vague and does not really mean anything.

> I enjoy playing football as a hobby and for personal achievement; I also remain very popular amongst my peers because I happen to look very much like Wayne Rooney.

✗ Not really relevant to the student's university application. If it is an attempt to be amusing it doesn't work. It is safer to avoid flippancy.

> I am a focused person when I have the motivation, which I feel I would have as the subject is something I have genuine interest in and would want to pursue it further after graduating by becoming a PE teacher.

✗ This sentence implies that the student does not always have the motivation to study!

 **TOP TIPS**

**1** An interesting opening paragraph, which goes straight to the point

**2** Enthusiasm for the study of sports science and an understanding of the subject at degree level

**3** Give information about extracurricular activities and skills gained through them

 **THINGS TO AVOID**

**1** Spelling and punctuation mistakes: get your statement proofread carefully

**2** Outdated information: sporting activities from primary school are not relevant

**3** An interest in sport which does not go beyond watching it on TV

**4** Exaggerated claims: tell us about your achievements but don't make them up

**4** Show an interest in sport and exercise-related activities outside the classroom

**5** Show an awareness of the rigours of higher level studying and independent learning

**6** Demonstrate an ability to work well in practical classes and labs, as well as written and research skills

**5** Giving too much information about your social activities and hobbies: focus on information relevant to your intended courses

---

##  RECOMMENDED READING AND WEBSITES

▪ D Sewell, P Watkins, & M Griffin *Sport and Exercise Science: An introduction*, Holder Arnold, 2005

I am grateful to the university of Essex for their help in preparing this profile. Other highly rated courses can be found at the universities of Bath, Bournemouth, Loughborough, Leeds and Birmingham.

# THEATRE AND PERFORMANCE DESIGN AND TECHNOLOGY

**This academic profile was written by admissions tutors at the Liverpool Institute of Performing Arts (LIPA). The information is useful to all applicants, but some of the advice is pertinent to that department in particular.**

## SUBJECT OVERVIEW

The theatre and entertainments industries have a lot of employees who have never studied at university, and some areas such as the live sound industry are keen that all new staff start at the bottom and work their way up. So why would you want to study a degree before starting employment? At university, you should learn a broad base of skills as a technician or designer to give you the flexibility to work in a number of environments, whereas an employer might initially want you for a specific task and not give you the opportunities to try new tasks. You may not need to start at the very bottom as a graduate, and you are much more likely to rise a lot faster even if you do. You may also hit a 'glass ceiling' as a non-graduate where some organisations will only offer their more senior positions to applicants with a degree.

# WHAT SKILLS OR ATTRIBUTES DO ADMISSIONS TUTORS LOOK FOR IN A GOOD APPLICANT?

Academically, we are looking for people with five GCSE passes at a minimum grade of C or above, including English. In terms of level 3 qualifications we don't specify which subjects you need to study – we are looking for people who achieve a minimum of 160 UCAS tariff points, which should ideally be attained in one of the following ways:

- grade C and C at A level or AVCE level. All A level subjects accepted, excluding General Studies
- 'merit, pass, pass' profile at BTEC National Diploma level
- all equivalent UK and overseas qualifications are also accepted, including Welsh Baccalaureate, Scottish Highers, Welsh, European and International Baccalaureate and Irish Leaving Certificate.

These requirements will differ depending on the university and course. For the design degree, we normally expect applicants to also successfully complete a foundation studies course in art and design or an equivalent course at pre-degree level. We are also interested in your experience to date in the subject, your interdisciplinary interest, your communication skills and enterprise.

In terms of personality traits, we look for people who are excited about studying the subject. A hunger to learn more and keep learning as your career goes on is important to us. You do not necessarily have to be an expert because if you are you may have nothing left to learn. You need to be good at talking about your own experience and what you have learnt from it and good at analysing your own strengths and weaknesses. You do not have to be perfect – what could we add to that?

A good sense of humour helps – you can be working for long hours, often under pressure with lots of different personalities.

You do not have to be a show-off but you must not be afraid to speak your mind. You will need some kind of independence to take on this degree course and must not be afraid to ask questions if you do not understand something (much better than pretending that you do know something when you don't).

You do not have to be a happy, smiley person about everything – but if you come in and complain about the course you're on at the moment or things you have done in the past, you may come across as a negative person who may struggle to enjoy anything.

Your enthusiasm should show itself in being able to describe what you like in a variety of different ways.

## WHAT DOES A GOOD PERSONAL STATEMENT LOOK LIKE?

You need to show enthusiasm, coupled with a clear idea of where you want to go in the future and why this type of course might help you get there or narrow down your choices. It would help if you explain why studying at university is important as well as why you just want to study the subject itself.

### Example from a good Personal Statement

> At the moment I'm on an art and foundation course and have a big interest in 3-D design and often try to combine my techniques from all areas, using my knowledge of structure to design and make extravagant garments. I especially enjoy working on combining materials such as wire, metal and wood with fabric. I have learnt how to manipulate material in different ways. I like experimenting with different

techniques to produce different looks. I have had the opportunity to work in a wide variety of materials and styles and have been encouraged to be more creative and independent in my work. In my courses I particularly enjoy 'realisation', where I actually make my final design. It is the most exciting section of the coursework. And also the design process where I illustrate and explore media to record ideas. It is very satisfying when you can see how you have come to produce this final item.

I find contextual studies very interesting as I get a chance to explore and admire other artists' work, observing how their work relates to things around us. During these last two years of my studies I have built up a knowledge of other artists. In particular, in my third year I have begun to create a personal sketch book of information and creativity of artists whose work inspires me by visiting galleries and other sources.

✓ In this statement, the applicant describes what they are doing now with enthusiasm and talks about developing these skills further in ways that are relevant to our course.

One of the main reasons why a Personal Statement might not work for would be if the candidate appears to be torn between two different career paths. For example, if you are applying to acting or directing courses and are also applying to a design/technology course that suggests you might not be all that committed to our course. Being a designer or technician is a career in itself and we want to know you are committed to that – not to see it as a pathway to a career in performing. In one Personal Statement someone commented that they were really looking forward to 'retail display design'. This was not the course that they were applying for at LIPA. Similarly, another candidate spoke about their love of teaching and the fact that they really want to work with primary school children. That is not part of our course, so that candidate is more likely to be better placed studying a focused educational degree. We do have some students whose career aspirations change while studying, but if you already know before starting university that you'd rather do something else then that's what you should be looking for in the courses you apply for.

These tips are from a student who is studying theatre and performance design at LIPA.

 **TOP TIPS**

**1** Get involved both in school and outside of school if you can

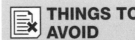 **THINGS TO AVOID**

**1** Complaining that you haven't had any opportunities up till now:

(try to explore opportunities to take part in local theatre): this will enable you to write about these experiences in the Personal Statement and sell your genuine interest in the subject

**2** Talk to people: both those who work on stage and backstage, about what happens behind the scenes. Their experiences and what you learnt from them can also provide vital evidence of your interest. Put this in your statement

**3** Try everything once: even if you don't carry on working on that element of the production in the future. Being able to understand everything that goes on in a theatre helps in the future. This willingness to try and not being afraid to ask is something that you should allude to in the statement and any interview you may be asked to attend

**4** Watch shows and performances: that is what you will work towards, so it is always good and satisfying to see the final results. If you see a show and want to comment about the set design in the statement, this would be good

**5** Draw, take photos and keep your show programmes. Keep a record of everything you do; otherwise you have got nothing to show for it. Bring this to any interview you may have

life is what you make it! A good Personal Statement needs to reflect the fact that you have seen productions and done interesting things, so start now!

**2** Thinking that musical theatre in the West End is the only successful or interesting type of show going on

**3** Being an anorak: having a passion for something is more relevant to us than knowing every serial number or model number

**4** Concentrating your design work into fashionable or niche areas such as pictures of fairies or angels: try and show a breadth of your interest and a range of different applications in the statement or portfolio you bring to university

**5** Poor spelling, grammar and punctuation. This is just lazy and shows that you are not really serious. If in doubt, get your statement and application proofread by a good teacher, tutor or friend

# RECOMMENDED READING AND WEBSITES

■ Gary Thorne, *Stage Design: A Practical Guide*, Crowood Press, 1999

I am grateful for the support I received from LIPA (www.lipa.ac.uk) in the preparation of this profile. Other highly rated courses can be found at the universities of Edge Hill, Canterbury Christ Church and Bath Spa.

# TOURISM MANAGEMENT

**This academic profile was written by an admissions tutor at Surrey University. The information is useful to all applicants, but some of the advice is pertinent to Surrey in particular.**

## SUBJECT OVERVIEW

Tourism is an activity of increasing economic consequence in the world and makes important contributions to gross national product, foreign currency earnings and employment. It also has both positive and negative social and environmental impacts and can contribute to poverty reduction. Because of this, universities have increasingly become interested in the management and understanding of tourism.

# WHAT SKILLS OR ATTRIBUTES DO ADMISSIONS TUTORS LOOK FOR IN A GOOD APPLICANT?

There are no specific academic subjects that are prerequisites for studying tourism. More important are an interest and passion for the subject and evidence that you can benefit from a university course. The industry stereotype is for extrovert, fun-loving personality types – but there are also many opportunities for more introverted, studious applicants!

Clearly the teaching styles will vary from department to department; however, at Surrey we would expect to offer contact time of 12–18 hours per week. As the subject is relatively new, teaching and learning styles tend to be dynamic and innovative. Many courses include a field trip abroad. Assessment is generally mixed including exams, coursework, projects and group work.

# WHAT DOES A GOOD PERSONAL STATEMENT LOOK LIKE?

A good Personal Statement has a clear structure with an introduction, a number of clearly explained and relevant points and a conclusion. It is well written, with correct grammar and spelling and without repetition. It effectively links your background, achievements, experience and interests to the course for which you have applied and it shows that you have undertaken some research into the subject area and into the nature of education at university level. It also shows that you have wider interests and achievements than those solely related to the course for which you have applied, and ideally you should show that you have critical and analytical abilities. With these in mind the structure is likely to include:

- information about you and your interests and ambitions
- your present studies and how these relate to your study and longer-term ambitions
- your particular achievements
- your broad understanding and knowledge of your planned field of study
- why you are interested in it
- how you feel you would contribute to the field
- critical awareness of an issue or issues related to tourism and an ability to analyse the issue.

 **TOP TIPS**

**1** Make sure that your statement has a clear structure with an introduction, a number of clearly explained and relevant points and a conclusion

 **THINGS TO AVOID**

**1** Poor spelling, punctuation and grammar

**2** A statement that lacks clarity and direction

**2** Have clear goals and make them clear in your statement

**3** Your statement must be well written, with correct grammar and spelling and without repetition

**4** Link your background, achievements, experience and interests to the course for which you have applied, and show that you have undertaken some research into the subject area and into the nature of education at university level

**5** You must also show that you have wider interests and achievements than those solely related to the course for which you have applied and ideally you should show that you have critical and analytical abilities

**3** A statement that does not refer to your academic skills and extracurricular interests

**4** A statement that shows little evidence of an understanding of business and the tourism industry in general

## RECOMMENDED READING AND WEBSITES

- The Tourism Society: www.tourismsociety.org

I am grateful to the department at the University of Surrey (www.surrey.ac.uk) for their support in compiling this profile. Other highly rated courses can be found at the universities of Bath Spa, Brighton, Exeter, Kent and Liverpool John Moores.

# VETERINARY SCIENCE

This academic profile was written by an admissions tutor at Nottingham University Veterinary School, which is newest of all the schools, having opened in 2006. The information is pertinent to all applicants but please be aware that some advice is relevant to this department alone.

## SUBJECT OVERVIEW

Studying veterinary medicine and science will allow you to gain the professionally recognised qualification, which will allow you to practise as a veterinary surgeon. Making the decision to become a veterinary surgeon will set you on a course for one of the most varied and exciting careers available. The veterinary profession offers many diverse and stimulating career opportunities combined with the privilege of working with animals.

Only seven institutions offer veterinary medicine in the UK – Bristol, Cambridge, Edinburgh, Glasgow, Liverpool, London (Royal Veterinary College) and Nottingham. Competition is high, but it is a myth that you need to be exceptionally academic.

## WHAT SKILLS OR ATTRIBUTES DO ADMISSIONS TUTORS LOOK FOR IN A GOOD APPLICANT?

Academically you should be able to show good overall achievement at GCSE level, including high grades in science subjects. At A2 level, normally most vet schools would expect students to have studied biology and chemistry, and be able to achieve high grades in these subjects. There are now other entry routes into vet school including the preliminary year at Nottingham (which accepts students with high grades in non-science or vocational subjects). There are also widening participation courses specifically aimed at learners from under-represented groups, such as the Gateway course run at RVC and Veterinary Science Certificate course at Lincoln (for progression to Nottingham) – these courses generally look for grades CCC at A2 level.

As a vet you will need good communication skills – listening, writing and speaking and motor skills such as good hand-eye co-ordination, dexterity and precision of motor skills. All vet schools will expect that you have gained some animal-focused work experience, preferably in a range of animal-related areas such as at a veterinary practice, working with horses or on a farm, at a zoo or wildlife park, in research or laboratory settings and spending time at an abattoir. You would be expected to have an understanding of the positive and negative aspects of a veterinary career and have an awareness of current important issues and developments in veterinary medicine and science.

It is important that you possess a number of personal attitudes and attributes that are needed to both be successful on the course and in a veterinary career including a caring ethos (compassion, tolerance, patience, empathy) and a sense of social responsibility. You should be able to cope with change and uncertainty and to overcome challenges while understanding your own limitations. Schools expect applicants to possess self-motivation, self-confidence, self-reliance and initiative. You should be able to show that you have the ability to work independently and as part of a team, integrate, co-operate and be flexible. Good personal organisational skills and time management skills are a must.

## WHAT DOES A GOOD PERSONAL STATEMENT LOOK LIKE?

A good Personal Statement will cover why you want to study veterinary medicine and science, detailing your experience gained to date and your understanding of the profession.

Admissions tutors would like to see some evidence of work experience where you came into contact with animals. This needs to be at least two weeks in length and references may be taken. Taster courses such as VETSIX are popular and useful but not obligatory. Mention the aspects of your A levels (or equivalent) that you have found particularly interesting. Describe any coursework you have completed and any books that you have read that may be relevant. Please do not lie, as this will become clear at interview!

Your statement should cover personal responsibilities and leadership, and any achievements and awards won, and an indication of how these relate to competences required of a veterinary surgeon. Needless to say, structure and organisation, grammar and spelling are also important.

Although your Personal Statement is important, most schools will have additional methods of assessment including the Biomedical Admissions Test (BMAT – www.admissionstests.cambridgeassessment.org.uk/adt/bmat), online questionnaires and work experience references.

## TOP TIPS

**1** Say why you want to study veterinary medicine and science

**2** Detail your experience gained to date and your understanding of the profession

**3** Emphasise the work experience early on and explain what you learnt as well as what you did

**4** Taster courses such as VETSIX are popular and useful, but not obligatory

**5** Mention the aspects of your A levels (or equivalent) that you have found particularly interesting

## THINGS TO AVOID

**1** Having a rose-tinted picture of the profession: it will include working at night, in all conditions and you will be paid as much as a medic! Show that you understand this in your statement and interview

**2** Poor spelling, grammar and punctuation

## RECOMMENDED READING AND WEBSITES

- The Royal College of Veterinary Surgeons (www.rcvs.org.uk) produces a free leaflet called *Training to Become a Veterinary Surgeon*

I am grateful to Nottingham University Veterinary School (www.nottingham. ac.uk/vet) for their support in compiling this profile.

Here are some excellent books, journals or websites that you might like to use to help with your research. This is not an exhaustive list. New books are written and websites created every month. These are the ones that I have found most helpful and they are all currently on sale or available online.

# GOOD UNIVERSITY GUIDES

There are many of these guides in the bookshops. Some are better than others and below you will find my personal top five that ought to be in every library. If not, ask for them to be bought or get hold of one of them for your own use!

### The Guardian University Guide
*Guardian Books*

Packed with no-nonsense advice, the *Guardian University Guide* takes prospective students through every process they will encounter when entering further education. It is updated annually and the subject ratings are up to date and based on the UCAS tariff.

### The Times Good University Guide
*Times Books*

This is also updated annually and is available online. Although formal in style, it does offer sound and unbiased advice. It also has a league table to help differentiate between the quality of departments in the various universities and colleges.

### The Virgin Alternative Guide to British Universities
*Virgin Books*

This guide was favourably reviewed by the *Times Educational Supplement* and *Careers Adviser* magazine. It is written in a more informal style with regular contributions from real students. As well as offering a comprehensive guide to all the major UK universities, it also looks at aspects of student life that other sources ignore. For instance, the reader can discover where to find the best discounts, the best pubs and the best second-hand books.

### Which Uni? Find the Best University for You
*Trotman Publishing*

This book helps you establish your priorities for choosing a university and match them to the institutions. It does this by rating universities on everything from the quality of the teaching to its facilities and the entertainment it has to offer, as well as student prospects after graduation.

# ALTERNATIVE GUIDES

Many universities now produce alternative prospectuses and guides. These are written by students, for students and are not always endorsed by the college authorities. While they will promote the university, they do offer an insight into the day-to-day life of a student that you will not find elsewhere. One site that offers a 'one-stop shop' approach is www.whatuni.com, where current students post comments about the university where they are studying.

Most of these guides are available online. You can usually find them with Google or Yahoo, using the search words.

# GENERAL GUIDES TO SUBJECTS AND COURSE REQUIREMENTS

### 'Getting into' course guides

*Trotman Publishing*

Each title in this series, which is updated regularly, provides an unbiased and frank insight into what it is like to study each subject at university, how to impress at interview, current issues that are pertinent to the subject and advice about which university to choose.

The range of titles on offer includes Art and Design, Law, Medicine, Physiotherapy, Psychology and Business Management.

### Getting into Oxford and Cambridge

*Trotman Publishing*

Updated annually this is a well-written book that offers the potential Oxbridge applicant an insight into the world of Oxford and Cambridge. It contains detailed advice on all the undergraduate colleges and courses and how to decide which to apply for. It explains the application procedure clearly, debunks the myths that persist and offers an insight into the interviews that seem to lie at the heart of most peoples' concerns. It does not attempt to pretend that there is some secret code that you need to learn to win a place.

In my experience, the candidates who win a place from my school tend to be those who are first-class, straight A-grade academics who are obsessively passionate about their subject. Bright sixth formers do not always demonstrate a passion for a subject to an admissions tutor, which is why, so often, they fail to receive a conditional offer. The days of getting in because your parents and grandparents went to the same institution are essentially over.

### HEAP: Choosing your Degree Course & University
*Trotman Publishing*

A companion to the *HEAP 2011: University Degree Course Offers* book below, this one takes each subject of study and outlines what the key universities in that field offer in terms of courses. A good book to use to narrow down your course choices and get a sense of the different options open to you around the UK.

### HEAP 2011: University Degree Course Offers
*Trotman Publishing*

This book is one of the best known in the higher education world. Edited by Brian Heap, it is annually updated and provides the most comprehensive single source for subject specific information available. Students can find out about and research a range of subjects, including offers most commonly made in each university, information about interviews, open days and the number of applicants who apply per place.

## WEBSITES
### General education

These are websites whose aim it is to provide information to students starting out on their journey towards a successful UCAS or CUKAS application. These are all currently available online and their content evolves on a daily basis.

### Centigrade
*www.coa.co.uk/centigrade*

COA is a leading provider of careers and higher education information to schools and colleges in the UK and overseas. Its Centigrade programme is endorsed by UCAS and used by many schools as a test to match students' interests with higher education courses. The test can now be conducted online and the student will receive a report and copy of the COA Careers Directory.

## CUKAS

*www.cukas.ac.uk*

This is a relatively new site that is managed by UCAS. Conservatoires UK Admissions Service (CUKAS) is the music conservatoire equivalent of UCAS. Currently the following conservatoires accept applications through this online method.

- Birmingham Conservatoire — www.conservatoire.bcu.ac.uk
- Leeds College of Music — www.lcm.ac.uk
- Royal College of Music — www.rcm.ac.uk
- Royal Northern College of Music — www.rncm.ac.uk
- Royal Scottish Academy of Music and Drama — www.rsamd.ac.uk
- Royal Welsh College of Music and Drama — www.rwcmd.ac.uk
- Trinity College of Music — www.tcm.ac.uk

### Hot Courses

*www.hotcourses.com*

A good search engine for courses at university and college.

### Push Online

*www.push.co.uk*

This is the main Push site and well worth a visit.

## UCAS

*www.ucas.com*

The UCAS website remains the primary portal of choice for students. The site has developed significantly in the last few years and now offers a diverse range of research tools. The most obvious is the Course Search function leading to the UCAS Entry Profiles. It also has a free questionnaire produced by COA called the Stamford Test. This is a slimmed-down version of Centigrade and one of the activities in this publication involves students undertaking this test.

## Newspapers

Other excellent sources of general information available online include the two best newspaper education sites – Guardian Education (www.education.guardian.co.uk) and Times Online (www.timesonline.co.uk).

Both provide excellent information that ranks universities and departments according to a range of criteria. As with all league tables, they need to be treated with caution. However, they are free and well respected by the careers staff that I meet.